YOUNGER & WISER

A Collection of Backstory Poetry and Inspirational Prose

www.youngerandwiser.net

Published in the United States of America

ISBN: 0998324000
ISBN 13: 978-0-9983240-0-5

Library of Congress Control Number: 2016910033

Dreamquest Publishing
A Division of Royal Production Services, Inc.
Katonah, New York

Interior Design: Nancy Parsons

Dedicated to the creative spirit
that simmers within every human soul

Younger & Wiser

CONTENTS

INTRODUCTION TO BACKSTORY POETRY

When reading the poetry of others, I frequently suffer a sense of incompletion. Even the most profound poems often leave me wondering how to interpret the author's words. While appreciating the freedom to apply my own mental machinations to the thrust of someone else's creative writing, I usually end up staring longingly at most poetry, wishing there was an opportunity to ask each poet what he or she was really thinking, and what circumstances germinated each creation. Since every poem arises from some alchemical combination of experiences and cerebral connections in an author's mind, it can be concluded that every poem has a story. Numerous conversations with other writers have taught me the genesis of a literary work is often more fascinating than the work itself.

There has always been a nagging voice in the back of my brain urging me to make the creative process more transparent. One summer afternoon, while I sat in my backyard, an idea bolted into my cortex. The thunderbolt commanded me to write a companion backstory for a poem written about my father's premature demise. Obeying the command, I grabbed a sheet of paper and began recounting my surroundings when the poem *Father's Day on Christmas* was written, a moment permanently seared into my memory as a mental tattoo. Immediately after finishing my first backstory, floods of memories recalling inspirations for other poems began sloshing around in my mind. One by one, each demanded to have a voice, and a radically revised format for this book emerged. The three main guidelines utilized in developing backstories for *Younger & Wiser* are:

Describe the circumstances that inspired the poem,
Clarify my state of mind at the moment of inspiration
Share some wisdom phrases relevant to the poem

By no means are backstories intended to dictate the reader's interpretation of any poems.

Meshing backstories with poetry inadvertently opened a portal to a parallel universe of literary expression. Having entered that galaxy, I cannot imagine going back. Backstory poetry merges my love of cinema with my love of contemporary poetic expression. When sprinkled into the poetry genre, backstories facilitate greater freedom of style by providing additional avenues to illuminate context without diverting a poem's structure, similar to the role of backstories in films. The movie industry has demonstrated how vivid and intimate life experiences can flow through a backstory, providing essential information about a movie's plot and characters.

Backstories also provide foundations for the deep-rooted subconscious desire most authors and artists have to achieve complete self-expression. As this literary concept is explored further, hopefully backstories will serve as potent communication vehicles capable of enriching the poetry experience for authors as well as readers. With this added dimension of expression, poetry books will possess the more dynamic qualities of poetry readings. The implementation of backstories as poetic companions has the potential to spark deeper cerebral conversations between writers and readers, paving the way for poetry to become a more mainstream art form. My fundamental goal when writing backstory poetry is to establish a meaningful conversation between my written words and each reader's mind. It is my belief that if backstory poetry gains popularity, it will certainly provide fertile ground for such conversations, as well as diverse literary innovation.

Not every entry in this book is partnered with a backstory. That is by design. Some poems simply shot from head to pen without noteworthy circumstance. A few leaped from heart to page in an emotional blur, while other poems are short and self-explanatory.

In the final analysis, history is the backstory of human existence. Both history and backstory contain the word "story" and stories breathe life into mere facts. We are constantly reminded that history does repeat itself. Unfortunately, such repetition doesn't guarantee the learning of any lessons.
This has become mankind's supreme challenge:

To figure out the lessons of history and move in a more sensible direction.

Encouraging such thinking is one of my main reasons for assembling this book, as I have attempted to dissect my life experiences to ascertain universal truths, hoping the tales of my personal odyssey will benefit others.

Younger & Wiser

CRY LIKE A MAN

Today I sat down
    and cried like a man.
I cried for all
    who will never know
        the pleasures of a good home,
    for people who love objects
        more than themselves
...and as my tears poured down
        upon the shadow of an ant,
I cried for those who live so loud
    they cannot hear the sounds of love,
        dreams that never come true,
        and all endangered species

I cried for technology
  while praying for wisdom
    to guide our hazardous course
I cried for the ocean
    the air
    fragile forests
    infants
    the old
    the sick
    the wealthy and the poor
who all find their own ways to suffer

Where does it all end?
    These tragedies seem so far away
        but I just can't stop crying
            when there is so much to cry about.
It's really not the world
    but the people,
        not just who they are
            but what they will become

Once a boulder starts rolling down a hill
    it becomes impossible to bring back to the top,
so today I sat down
    and cried for my father
        who despite his greatness
            died before he could tell me
about the last time
    he sat down
        and cried like a man

BACKSTORY
Cry Like A Man

Cry Like A Man is about mourning the death of a parent, and exploring deep compassion for human suffering. A convergence of these two powerful forces gripped me one chilly winter afternoon, creating an urge to channel the grief derived from my father's sudden demise into an all-encompassing world view. Such a vision provided plenty to cry about, but nothing boils my blood faster than the stinging loss of my father when I was a very young man. It is a nagging grief that haunts me at will with surprise attacks triggered by seemingly innocuous events. For some reason, I cannot cry sufficiently when standing up, so these attacks always cause me to sit down before tears are able to flow. Transitioning the focus of my emotional core from grief to compassion initiated a rapid healing process.

The backstory for Cry Like A Man was inspired by the movie *October Sky*, a film telling the true story of Homer Hickam. Homer was a teenager whose adventures launching rockets led him to become a NASA rocket scientist. A powerful subplot of *October Sky* is the turbulent relationship between Homer and his father. Father-son relationships in movies always capture my heart. *October Sky* introduces Homer as a young boy growing up in a close-knit mining community dominated by the local coal mine. Inspired by Russia's launch of the Sputnik satellite, Homer develops an unbridled passion for rockets. His father is a life-long employee of the local mining company who wants Homer to follow in his footsteps. Fortunately, Homer is strong-willed and highly motivated. His unwavering determination brings ardent support from friends, teachers and numerous townspeople, but never from Homer's father.

Affectionately nicknamed "rocket boy" by supporters, Homer wins the national science fair with his brilliant rocket project and returns home a hero. His climactic demonstration of rocketeering prowess finally gains his father's approval. The long overdue father-son embrace left me in a puddle of my own tears as it revived the final time my father told me how much he loved me. This resurrection of grief rose up from deep inside and circulated through my body like an out-of-control forest fire. A flood of memories about my dad overwhelmed me, instantly linking *October Sky* to Cry Like a Man.

After studying this poem and its backstory, a significant insight emerged. I realized full immersion in grief is capable of yielding very positive outcomes. Allowing grief to fully run its course paves the way for an emergence of clarity and compassion. As clarity and compassion grow, happiness and joy can return. Concern for humanity, although a very serious matter, also provides infinite avenues for joyous deeds. The magnificent transition from grief to joy represents one of humanity's finest attributes. Although Cry Like A Man was originally inspired by personal tragedy, substantial catharsis was derived from adopting a universal view of human suffering. Fittingly, I began writing this poem with tears of grief, and finished it with tears of joy.

EDUCATED SWEAT

After years of having much
    but wanting more,
too often pouring every ounce
into a seemingly precious pitcher
only to discover gaping holes in unsuspected places,
after watching a mockery made of caring,
it finally dawns on my educated sweat
    that everything is something,
something can be nothing,
but
nothing is everything

The events of life
parallel the ingestion of food
where no meal
    is great enough
to eliminate the need for another

So when desire strikes
I don't put on my best clothes anymore,
        having learned
the highest mountain peak
is merely the bottom of the sky
        and
success can be the ultimate disappointment

BACKSTORY
Educated Sweat

Although I wrote Educated Sweat more than thirty years ago, it still resonates with me today. After surviving many more life experiences, I still agree with its conclusion: Fulfillment and happiness are not necessarily achieved by effort alone, and apparent success can often feel empty. It takes awareness and other intangibles to create a rewarding and happy life.

The backstory for Educated Sweat proved difficult to write. It truly made me sweat, mainly because no single event inspired its creation. But then I had a change of heart. Something began urging me to forge ahead. I spent a substantial amount of time beating myself up for not being able to concoct any worthy embellishment or insight to highlight my original words. Meanwhile, an irate voice in my mind was shouting,

"How could you have lived another thirty years and not learned anything worth mentioning about this poem?"

To which I silently shouted back,

"Maybe I was wiser than I realized when I was younger!"

This internal dispute raged inside my head for days. I repeatedly studied every word of Educated Sweat as if reviewing a crucial legal document. What I concluded from this monumental struggle was, in some ways I was very wise at a young age, but in other ways I was clueless—a dichotomy that eventually evolved into the title of this book.

So here is my updated lesson regarding Educated Sweat:
Apply the concept of *"sweating smart"* to avoid many perilous pitfalls of life. Always provide your instincts some space to evolve, and most importantly,

"Never sweat in vain."

WORM'S EYE VIEW

How does one determine the value of a life?
An earthworm spends his eternity beneath the ground.
Without eyes,
he never sees the beauty of this world
and after a brief tenure of inspired subterranean wiggling,
an earthworm's fury fades without a peep

His uneventful death leaves him decomposing
to enrich the very soil
in which he has mindlessly toiled,
leaving our Earth a slightly better place

Collectively, billions of earthworms
continually enrich our planet,
helping bear fruit that feeds
immense populations parading on its surface

Meanwhile, the world's greatest man
in his finest moment of glory
changes the course of human history
but unknowingly pollutes the deteriorating environment
with his daily waste

His demise, although gloriously commemorated
by a thousand trumpets,
is unfortunately of no nutritional value
to the small piece of real estate
his coffin will occupy for centuries

Collectively, millions of great men
pose a serious threat
to our increasingly fragile environment

No historian will ever proclaim
the everlasting greatness of an earthworm,
but when judged
by the Supreme Court of another consciousness,
one earthworm is clearly more valuable
in preserving the health of our wounded planet
than the greatest of men

BACKSTORY
Worm's Eye View

It may be doubted whether any other animals
have played so important a part in the history of the world
as have these lowly creatures called worms.
—Charles Darwin

By sliding in their tunnels, earthworms act as an innumerable army of pistons pumping
air in and out of the soil on a 24-hour cycle.
—Bill Mollison

Worm's Eye View attempts to evaluate the life of worms in comparison to humans. Clearly, such analysis is a matter of perspective. It is rather sobering to realize if we take Mother Nature's point of view, a very different hierarchy might be operating here on Earth.

As a youth living in New York City, the only time I ever saw a worm was on a fishing boat. This limited view gave an impression worms were put on our planet for the sole purpose of helping humans catch fish. When I moved to the country, the omnipresence of worms aroused my curiosity. A bit of research educated me about their significant contributions.

Here is what I learned:
Surprisingly, even poor soil has 250,000 earthworms per acre, while fertile farmland may have as many as 1,750,000 per acre. Earthworms move by peristalsis, a burrowing motion that creates channels in the soil, thereby enabling improved aeration and drainage. Their ability to break down organic materials and excrete concentrated nutrients makes earthworms a key contributor in promoting the formation of nutrient-rich soil. This is why earthworms are often utilized to prepare tainted land for the return of healthy native ecosystems, which builds a powerful case for earthworms in the trial of Worm vs. Human.

Worm's Eye View shifted my outlook on worms and funerals significantly. The words "decomposing to enrich the very soil" stuck in my mind, inspiring the creation of Composted.

COMPOSTED

The smell of death is never pretty
whether it be rodent
    human,
or once-fragrant rose,
the stench of a creature's demise
never does it justice
nor do gourmet meals retain appeal
when left to decay overnight

This obvious truth
struck me as significant
upon viewing one recently dead squirrel
splattered across a city street

My mind flashed back to the day before
that squirrel was flattened by a truck's massive tire
whose imprint was now permanently tattooed
across its little squirrel body

Retro vision confirmed
just days ago
this was a squirrel with hopes and dreams,
happily dining on a sumptuous walnut,
one of many
stored in his secret underground vault

When squirrel perished suddenly
there was no notification of next of kin,
no eulogy to commemorate his accomplishments,
no stoppage of nature to enshrine
    the magnificence of this once proud animal
now offered to Mother Earth as compost
for an endless chain of existence
that transforms death's stench
into life's next intoxicating aroma

Sharpening an ice cream stick found littering the sidewalk,
I ceremoniously dug squirrel
    a parkside grave,
wishing him well next time around
while I wondered
what the scene will look like
when it is my turn to be composted

BACKSTORY
Composted

Take only what you need, and leave the land as you found it.
—Arapaho proverb

I have occasionally imagined what my funeral will look like. With eyes tightly shut, I try to picture the small crowd that gathers and eavesdrop on what they are saying. My mind's eye conjures up a bleak rainy afternoon in a muddy cemetery with all attendees mumbling unintelligibly.

Composted concentrates on posthumous existence, attempting to analyze the inevitable physical decay that occurs after the end of life. For no particular reason, the squirrel emerged as creature of choice, probably because squirrels are one of the few undomesticated animals frequently visible in an urban environment. Ascribing human protocols to the death of a squirrel seemed almost as absurd as ascribing protocols of the wild to a human death, yet both are possible within the spectrum of existence since all living organisms are part of the endless perpetual cycle of life, death and rebirth.

This cycle has always fascinated me, as I often ponder how each living organism eventually decomposes and becomes part of the world's food chain, implying every decomposed human has been indirectly consumed by other creatures or ingested by a plant. Perhaps an ancient ancestor's DNA has been eaten by a cow my butcher slaughtered to sell me a steak. The same holds true for creatures of the sea, birds, and the complete cornucopia of living beings since the beginning of time. Allowing my imagination to run wild, I wonder if I have digested a few particles of dinosaur, or even Leonardo da Vinci's brain.

Is it possible decomposed brain matter can resurface through this process? Perhaps this is why so many wild ideas populate my mind. Armed with newly acquired knowledge about the value of earthworms, I remain hopeful my remains will somehow enrich some soil to benefit those still living.
If that means I must be composted, then so be it!

9/11 SYNDROME

We give money
but it's not enough

We volunteer
but it's not enough

We send canned food to Africa,
we hug firemen
but it's still not enough

Every television torments us
with images of billowing smoke
and endless replays of airplanes
crashing into the Trade Center,
while aerial views of Ground Zero
tell us our souls are still roasting
in that pile of rubble

As we mourn the dead and injured,
we also mourn the safety we once felt
while absorbing the shocking realization
we are so vulnerable

We can't escape,
we don't want to escape,
part of us is still smoldering
deep underground

We want to be there,
we sense our world is spiraling out of control,
the hero in us aches to contribute
as voices inside scream
 "How should we respond?"

BACKSTORY
9/11 Syndrome

We cannot solve the significant problems we face today
on the same level we were on when we created them.
—Albert Einstein

Breathe in the sorrows of the world, and breathe out compassion.
—The Buddha

9/11 Syndrome was written shortly after the 9/11 attack on the World Trade Center. At that time I was living in Manhattan and experienced firsthand this tragedy from within the traumatized fishbowl while also being barraged daily by horrific images of destruction repeatedly presented on television.

The air in Manhattan was thick and acrid for weeks. The Broadway theater district where I frequently worked was temporarily a ghost town. It was eerie to pass through Times Square and not see any people milling around. Everyone sensed a seismic shift in the world, and the phrase *"Ground Zero"* was most appropriate for every shell-shocked New Yorker.

As the city staggered along struggling to restore some degree of normalcy, I decided to step back and take a global glance at what was transpiring, hoping to figure out what needed to be done. 9/11 incited an extended period of raw emotion that permanently changed life as we knew it. Like a bookmark, this tragic event separated two eras in national and world history. It also highlighted a number of long-simmering issues in desperate need of resolution.

9/11 left our nation's foreign policy in a state of confusion. In attempting to extricate the country from this tragedy, our leaders depended on the fallacious logic proclaiming,
> *"An enemy of my enemy is my friend"*.

After analyzing numerous world events in the post 9/11 era, an alternate view arose from my contemplation:
> *"An enemy of my enemy may also be my enemy"*

SKETCH

The old man
sits on a porch stoop
holding his gray cat

The scene doesn't look like much,
but his unshaven face and tattered trench coat
speak the many winding roads
    of his past sixty years,
those he loved, then lost
    those who loved him
      yet were abandoned by his once carefree heart,
wealth gained and squandered
friends who died too young,
    the dream country house he never owned

Faces don't wrinkle
solely from passage of time.
A man earns his wrinkles
    with mistakes and disappointments
inevitable though avoidable they may be

This man owned a dog once,
    a trusted dog
who ate at the dining room table
    listening carefully to endless gory details.
That dog knew everything,
except how to speak and play poker,
        but dog lives are short
so after a canine funeral
    which lasted twenty years,
the man bonded with stray cats
    trained to listen to what was left:
      chilling stories of stray animals
who all have tragic tales of their own to tell
    but sadly swallow them in solitary silence

So it is the summation of a life
to see not much
as the old man sits on a porch
with his gray cat

BACKSTORY
Sketch

The experience of writing Sketch felt like drawing a picture with a pencil. I wrote this poem in front of my apartment in Santa Monica, California. One late afternoon, as I returned home from the grocery store, a scraggly old man sat across the street on the stoop of a porch. Even though it was a very warm afternoon, this old man wore a tattered raincoat. He clearly had not shaved in many days and his hair was disheveled. Nested on the old man's lap was an equally disheveled gray cat. As the old man scratched between its ears, the cat squinted with pleasure. They both seemed at peace, indicating neither had anywhere else to go. This unglamorous duo caught my eye as I unloaded two large bags of groceries from my car and strolled toward my apartment door.

After taking a few steps, I was struck by an urge to capture this most mundane scene on paper. Inspired to attempt a verbal sketch, I quickly emptied one of my grocery bags, pulled out a pencil, and sat on the sidewalk directly facing the old man. He and his cat never took notice of me, and we never spoke a word to each other. The more I wrote on my brown paper palette, the more I felt I knew the old man. When I was done writing his verbal portrait, I reloaded the groceries and hurried home to study my sketch, which I envisioned in black and white.

I never saw that old man again. I can only assume he didn't live across the street and was just passing through. Perhaps he was homeless, and then again, perhaps he was a billionaire cat lover. No matter what his true condition in life was, Sketch is the essential reality his appearance conveyed to me in that moment.

SAVING SYLVIA PLATH

She belonged to Ted Hughes
    until he threw her back into the sea,
a glistening silver fish
    longing to swim
with all who encountered
    her brilliant words,
constantly suffering
    delectably demure
yet tragically unaware
    the navy of lifesavers
poised to save her tortured life

Our world is ill prepared
    to repair great beauty in distress,
as rapturous beauty
    terrifies even the most heroic
from attempted rescue
    due to fear of tarnishing
its wondrous fragile shell

One by one they froze in place
    awed by her exotic unreachable puzzle
zigzagging toward the inevitable precipice
    treacherous cliff of no return,
a black hole
sucking in wounded birds
swallowing full-grown dogs
family pets
marriages
houses and trees
  into a sensuous sea
    whose immense tongue
      licked delicious whipped-cream fantasies
while destroying a vulnerable life
    addicted to passion,
craving a taste of heaven on earth
    at any price

BACKSTORY
Saving Sylvia Plath

The courage of the poet is to keep ajar the door that leads into madness.
—Christopher Morley

My introduction to Sylvia Plath was the 2003 movie titled *Sylvia*, which featured Gwyneth Paltrow in the title role. Watching Sylvia Plath's rise to literary prominence and fall into the depths of depression rattled my soul. It also aroused my curiosity about this fascinating woman who was clearly a creative genius. I wanted to know more about her. I wanted to understand her and dig deeper into her mind. I also wanted to gain greater insight into the makeup of her husband, Ted Hughes. It was easy to figure out what brought these two titans of poetry together, but it was quite muddled as to what broke them apart. Did Ted Hughes leave Sylvia Plath because she was too crazy to live with, or was Ted a philandering poet preying on vulnerable impressionable women?

I immediately purchased one of Sylvia's poetry books. Then I bought one of Ted's books. Their poetry is sensational. Their lives were another story. To this day, I cannot say with any certainty I know what Ted Hughes was thinking when he began cheating on Sylvia. Judging from his behavior after Sylvia's suicide, it is obvious Ted loved her deeply until the day she died, even though he continued to be romantically involved with someone else. *Last Letter,* Ted Hughes's poem about Sylvia Plath's suicide, is gut wrenching. However, their love relationship seems to have been tinged with hints of tragedy from the very beginning.

Realizing I couldn't definitively solve the mystery of Sylvia Plath's love life, I began focusing on her thought process, as her many autobiographical writings reveal a brilliant but deeply troubled soul. I found her to be compelling and charismatic, the kind of sympathetic character a caring person would want to help. Knowing that Sylvia Plath attempted suicide prior to her betrayal by Ted Hughes lessens the blame history heaps on Ted's shoulders, but at the same time, her final successful suicide attempt was undeniably motivated in large part by the breakup of their relationship.

Two questions swirled in my mind:

-*Could anyone or anything have saved Sylvia Plath, and how many people tried but failed?*

-*Was her life a tragedy, or some kind of inscrutable meteor meant to shower us with her brilliant creations?*

I found myself longing to reach back in time and attempt to save her tortured soul. Since that heroic act was not possible, I wrote this poem in honor of her life.

FROSTED

This morning
you awaken
frosted as winter's window.
Iced with insecurity,
you nudge my sleep-ridden body
demanding a statement of eternal loyalty
after years of unspoken affection

Before I can roll over
you angrily rise and slam the door,
then begin your walk to nowhere
without letting me explain
a man feels more than he can say,
needing years of proper staging
to show the full dimensions of his heart

Since our first date
in the restaurant
where you squirted grapefruit in my eye,
I've wanted you to know
you are my definition of beauty
the light of my days and nights
my mother
father
dearest friend
and only lover,
my religion
    and eternal source of joy
for whom I would gladly sacrifice
more than I'll ever own

But most of all
I am smiling now
because by the door
    I notice
you left one silver shoe behind
and must return to hear my answer

BACKSTORY
Frosted

One morning I found myself in a very similar predicament to the person described in Frosted. The main thrust of this poem is the truth that men often have great difficulty expressing their loving emotions in an appropriate and timely fashion. This does not by any means imply men do not feel these emotions as strongly as women do.

Men tend to take actions that in their minds are making up for their lack of emotional expression. It took years of struggling with this issue to be able to verbally express my love and affection in ways that nurtured the soul of my loving partner. In truth, she is still teaching me this art. Fortunately, she was able to decipher my loving actions while I was learning how to fully express myself. The fact that the shoe left behind was one of her favorites definitely was an important factor at a critical junction in our relationship.

Frosted is actually a plea for female patience. Patience makes time your friend. If your love is true, your relationship will flourish. Time is not only a great healer; it can also provide endless opportunities for people to figure out how to love each other better. The reward is well worth the wait.

MEDITATION

Well, it finally happened
in the middle of a deep breath
never before sure
of love, life, or land
    this moment is mine

It exists just for now
only to flee and leave forever
disappearing with each tick of the transient clock

nothing can take away this feeling
so secure in knowledge
    am I
that my mission today
is to stand on this spot
at this time
    and *know*
instead of *wonder*
the infinite joy
of living in a moment

BACKSTORY
Meditation

Breathe. Let go. Remind yourself that this very moment
is the only one you know you have for sure.
—Oprah Winfrey

Without inner peace, it is impossible to have world peace.
—Fourteenth Dalai Lama

Places of extreme natural beauty provide ideal opportunities for rejuvenation. This poem was composed in Hawaii on a ledge as waves crashed into the side of a volcanic cliff below. There was something hypnotizing about the way spray from those waves floated up the barren black rock face to surround me in a gentle mist as I stood between colorful flowering bushes and palm trees. It was truly paradise, and I had it all to myself. While immersed in this lush environment, time seemed to stop. I felt the urge to stay forever, as the landscape's extreme harmony enabled my spirit to simultaneously relax and soar.

In those precious moments, I experienced a purely meditative state for the first time. Since then, meditation has become a daily ritual. Beyond spending time in pure thought, I attempt to maintain some degree of a meditative state at all times, since meditation's ultimate lesson teaches that mental clarity in all life situations is a key to being productive and fulfilled.

HERE AND THERE

There is always here.
If I want to go there
I start here

If I step toward there
it becomes here

When I get there
I am here

Always be here,
there will come

JOURNAL ENTRY

Intimate journal pages chronicle
   unbridled passion
      total chaos
trackless rollercoaster stampede
knows not where it wants to go
   finds no traction
     across bumpy roads
       filled with deadly obstacles

From below cracked pavement
    alluring fingers
point two ways to get nowhere
   along this weary path
  toward deserted ghost towns
    long since abandoned by those
who knew better than to embark upon
    journeys proven to devour their master

Why do I try?
   —because I must
Why must I?
   —because deep challenge gives as much as it takes away
Who cares?
   —I do, always
How do I know when I'm there?
   —it's the journey
How much is enough?
   —too much is still not enough
Who is this for?
   —all those who will listen
Why should they listen?
   —it might just enrich their lives
Why do I journal?
   —to share my struggles
What are my struggles?
   —my struggles are everyone's struggles
  everyone's struggles are my struggles,
      we are all connected
      we all can help
      we all need help
      never give up
      never stop caring
      never stop growing

breathe in
exhale
feel every moment,
then write it down
      so you can move on

BACKSTORY
Journal Entry

Poetry is the spontaneous overflow of powerful feelings.
It takes its origins from emotions recollected in tranquility.
—William Wordsworth

Journal Entry arose while vacationing at one of my favorite spa resorts. I noticed a journaling class on the morning events schedule. Not knowing what to expect, I trudged down to a cozy corner of the resort where about a dozen people gathered on some couches and comfortable chairs. After a brief greeting, the seminar instructor handed out beautiful leather-bound notebooks. With a minimum of guidance, we were instructed to journal about our stay at the resort. Obviously, I did not do the assignment correctly. My mind would not allow me to be so linear. After a few moments of confusion, I found myself evaluating my entire life. As my hand hovered over the lovely notebook, I hesitated to tarnish its virgin pages with the mess swirling in my head. As if standing naked at the edge of a freezing-cold lake, I was summoning up the gumption to dive in.

Finally, I couldn't procrastinate any longer. Allowing pen to touch paper without any idea what it might materialize, I was surprised to see the words "total chaos" appear on the page. A force from within took charge as if someone else was writing this piece for me, yet at the same time it was my truth. Journal Entry proceeded to capture the essence of my life, which is simultaneously turbulent, exhilarating, exasperating and surprisingly stable.

At the end of the journaling class, we were asked to read what we had written. When I read Journal Entry, it galvanized the whole group and led to some warm new friendships. An additional insight I gained from this experience is that heartfelt expressions of truth open the door to meaningful human interaction.

DREAM DIARY
Palm Beach, Florida/March 24, 1996

The dream begins:
I am sitting on a beach.
My fingers casually draw lines in the sand until I touch something that feels like the edge of a piece of clothing.
I tug on the piece of cloth, but it is difficult to lift.
I begin to dig at that spot to see what I have touched.
After a few moments of digging, I feel a body part attached to the cloth under the sand.
I am afraid to unearth it, but something tells me I must find out what, or who, is attached to the cloth.
Now digging fervently, I begin to uncover what appears to be a dead American Indian. His bronze-colored body is fully dressed and he has war paint on his face.
This terrifies me, so I quickly pour sand back on top of him so he may rest in peace, but…he moves!
The Indian isn't dead…he was merely asleep!
He sits up, sand cascading from his body as his torso rises.
Out of the corner of my eye, I notice a large snake rise from the high grass at the back edge of the beach.
I ask the snake:
>*"Is this Indian alone or is there a whole tribe buried underneath me?"*
The snake huddles with a tribe of snakes that suddenly appear between blades of high grass. After brief discussion, they all turn towards me. Instead of responding about the Indian, they tell me there is a big untruth in my life. It is not within me, but around me and it will soon reveal itself. This untruth will harm me but not ruin me, and I must learn forgiveness to resolve it fully.
The snakes conclude, *"Once you rid myself of this untruth, things will be better."*
The Indian stands up.
He opens his mouth slowly, then begins to speak.
He says it is time to get my life moving in a new direction.
The time is now to reach my potential, to *"quit pissing around."*
He tells me I don't know what I am doing in relationships with women:
>*"It is time to learn the art of how to love and be loved."*
A crowd begins to gather around the Indian and myself.
The Indian starts flapping his arms over his head, steadily increasing speed as if a bird readying for flight.
He tells me he owns the land we stand on. He says we can keep using the land as long as we *"do good for others."*
Otherwise, he warns, *"Someday we will take it back."*
Everyone on the beach flees in a panic.
I am alone with the Indian.
He continues flapping his arms, now more slowly as his flapping motion expands.
He tells me that the changes in my life have only just begun…

"What you do now will take years to come full circle, but there will be a powerful rebound after some time."

He raises both arms up in unison, extending upward as if reaching for the sky... his body takes on an angelic quality as his head looks skyward.

Lowering his gaze, he stares at me with his eyes on fire and says, *"I have spoken"*

His wrinkled face captivates me.

Like an extreme close-up, it keeps moving closer, his eyes penetrating my flesh as he steps toward me *and then dissolves into my body!*

It is a stunning feeling.

Suddenly, as if he has morphed into a second version of himself, he is also lying down in the sand with arms crossed and eyes closed, exactly as I found him.

The sand clears around and below him, causing his rigid body to sink straight down like a coffin being lowered into its grave.

As he sinks, sand instantly fills in over him, and he disappears.

I am shaken by his abrupt departure.

Staring alternately at his grave and then the sky, I ask,

"Is that it—Don't you have more to tell me?...Are you coming back?...Is that the whole lesson?...Have you actually merged into me?"

The Indian is gone. There are no more answers.

The ocean waves roar their approval.

The snakes disappear into the whistling grass.

I am alone on the beach.

A peaceful calm slowly sweeps over me as I close my eyes and debate which is more important: *writing this experience down, or taking in the moment.*

I choose to close my eyes, as I am still in the middle of a volatile circumstance.

While pondering the magnitude of this incredible experience, the lesson arrives:

My emotional self and intellectual self have been at odds for years, competing for time and attention. It is time to merge those two aspects into a more cohesive whole.

Inside, my eyes search for the Indian.

Upon opening my eyes, all I see is an empty sand beach.

I listen for the Indian's voice in the ocean breeze, but none is forthcoming.

I wonder if he is gone forever, or if he is still inside me.

The answer to this mystery may elude me for a lifetime.

Perhaps he has become my inner guide.

The process continues.

My new life begins.

I feel one step closer to the divine.

Will this dream ever end...will I ever wake up?

Well, I did wake up.

Before opening my eyes, I wanted to evaluate my physical condition.

I sensed I was sitting up with my back leaning on a rock.

My arms were collapsed down, and my fingers could feel sand between them.

My legs were extended out, heels in sand.

I slowly opened my eyes to find myself facing the ocean. Supporting me was the side of a large boulder on a beach. In back of the boulder was some high grass, very similar to the grass in my dream.

As I pressed my hands down to push my body up, my right hand slid a few inches to the right.

I looked down at my hand, and immediately broke into a cold sweat...there was a piece of cloth sticking up from the sand!

It looked like the same piece of cloth from my dream.

For a moment, I was afraid to move.

My fingers slowly wrapped themselves around the cloth.

My heart was racing.

I took a deep breath, not sure if I was about to slide into a living dream of no return.

Gripping tightly, I gave the piece of cloth a small tug.

To my great relief, the cloth released easily from the sand.

I exhaled and drew my arm toward my body, ready to toss the small piece of cloth back onto the beach, until out of the corner of my eye, I noticed a design in the cloth.

It was the same design as the Indian's outfit!

My mind entered a state of panic.

Was I dreaming, or was I awake?

Was I in the middle of a visionquest, or was I hallucinating?

Were supernatural forces descending upon me, or was this merely a bout of hyperactive imagination?

Was this some bizarre "rite of passage?"...and if so,

had I just become a Native American?

My hands were afraid to dig into the sand.

I stood up and looked around the beach

It was empty except for a passing seagull.

I heard a rustling in the high grass...something was moving in there...

Could it be the snakes?

Are our lives constantly surrounded by invisible forces?

Which is the dream—the life we live or the life we dream of, or are we all a part of someone else's dream?

This experience of shamanic alchemy lingers within me to this day.

For the past twenty years, my Indian friend has returned numerous times in unannounced dreams, floating through my mind at will.

Each visit is through a fog, never as clear as his first.

He never speaks, but his presence penetrates my core, resonating his original message more deeply each time.

The great untruth predicted in my dream revealed itself a few years after the snake's premonition. A business colleague harmed me but did not ruin me.

Without consciously remembering the snake's advice, I instinctively forgave the betrayal. That act of compassionate forgiveness has become one of my proudest moments, and surprisingly led to valuable new opportunities.

I also stopped *"pissing around"* with women and eventually married into deep love.

Was this dream a blessing or an omniscient warning...or have I been initiated into some higher spiritual realm?

All I know is, life has never been the same since March 24, 1996.

ARE WE THE GOATS?

Inside a darkened movie theatre
audiences cheer, as once again
the Earth is saved from alien invasion.
Miles away, using full moon's light
two hobos hop a freight train,
carrying their whole lives in wrinkled paper bags

An ocean swimmer screams to no avail
as a giant shark swallows his leg
while deep in the jungle
prehistoric tribes live on,
somehow finding reasons to exist
without assistance from therapists

Unconcerned,
thirsty camels search for water,
scouring desert sands without noticing
a herd of mountain goats look up in surprise
when the sky turns red

The goats grunt,
sounding universal calls of pain
uttered by a wounded species shortly before death.
Their mountaintop view is panoramic
as they shed tears that start a river.
The river grinds a path
toward a dam that lights a house
where a little boy trips and falls

His parents are away,
so he bleeds on the floor
until they come home
and frantically phone the family doctor, who is on vacation.
Their doctor finishes his game of tennis
then returns the call barely in time
to recommend a suitable place
for the youngster's funeral

The goats are afraid to shed more tears.
Instead, they go to sleep and dream of the past,
a past where change took centuries to be noticed.
These peaceful dreams are rudely interrupted
as a tractor transforms the lush valley below
into parking lots, while toppling trees
to print the local newspaper

The sky turns green.
The shark bites an ocean liner and breaks its jaw.
The desert becomes an inland sea, drowning every thirsty camel
while weeds sprout through deserted city streets
engulfing silent parking lots filled with abandoned cars.
The freight train rusts in its tracks

A stiff breeze blows open the hobo freight car
to find it empty,
the swimmer's body washes ashore.
Squinting from their mountaintop,
the goats suddenly realize
they are all alone

BACKSTORY
Are We The Goats?

A problem adequately stated is a problem well on its way to being solved.
—R. Buckminster Fuller

Whole societies have been reduced to ruin because they tolerated the intolerable.
—M. Scott Peck, *Abounding Grace*

*What most people don't seem to realize is that
there is just as much money to be made out of the wreckage of a civilization
as from the upbuilding of one.*
—Margaret Mitchell

Many days I am simply enthralled with the beauty of nature, imagining myself as one of the guardians of this wondrous world we live in. Sadly, in our contemporary world, awe-inspiring beauty often finds itself interspersed with ugliness and suffering.

Are We the Goats? was inspired by a visit to Waimea Canyon on the Hawaiian island of Kauai. Waimea Canyon is the largest canyon in the Pacific, and it is absolutely spectacular. The typical way to view this natural wonder is from a distance, as much of it is pristinely out of man's reach. There are a number of lookout points from which to view the canyon's amazing variety of colors and lush landscapes.

As I stood on a lookout peak about two miles from the actual canyon, I inadvertently looked down the slope below my side of the ridge. My heart sank as I witnessed mounds of garbage other tourists had carelessly thrown over the side of the cliff. The hillside was littered with empty grocery bags, aluminum cans, and all sorts of similarly ugly artifacts. It was an atrocity. I was disgusted by the scene, which resembled a landfill site in a big city. The dichotomy of such natural beauty blighted by human thoughtlessness overcame me, so I walked back to my rental car, hopped into the driver's seat, and began to write.

This poem is an attempt to focus public attention on the need to take better care of precious natural wonders we now know are so fragile. My hope is Buckminster Fuller's quote holds true, and mankind will make progress in this regard.

HISTORY IS LONG

History is long
the future is short

A world shivers,
mountains crumble
the earth cracks open
one oyster of truth at a time
while mankind's mistakes
pile up like mounds of garbage
at the beach

History is short
the future is long

This time a new species leads the parade
dancing over mounds of broken seashells
who remember nothing,
while once again the Earth seals its cracks
slowly building new beaches
for its next incarnation
to destroy

BACKSTORY
History Is Long

History never looks like history when you are living through it.
It always looks confusing and messy, and it always feels uncomfortable.
—John W. Gardner

History Is Long indirectly asks two intriguing questions:
"How many times has the Earth watched human life destroy itself?"
"What creatures have survived each apocalypse?"
Since I am not a paleontologist, I am forced to depend on the opinions of innumerable experts who have not yet discerned definitive evidence of rumored lost civilizations. Knowing all matter eventually decomposes leaves a door open to believing humankind has been through all this before, but the evidence was pulverized by the passage of time.

If one indulges in contemplating visions of pre-antiquity civilizations, then many questions follow. Certainly the nature of progress in every era must have had its unique events and details. It would be so helpful to know what extinguished each round of human existence, and how each successive human cycle resurrected itself. Even when studying historically recent developments, it seems such a pity the library at Alexandria, Egypt was torched by Roman conquerors, thereby destroying most records describing the evolution of ancient Egyptian culture.

If I were a historian, I would constantly be frustrated by the information not available to me. A nagging curiosity lingers, hinting history is much longer than any research has unearthed. While constantly keeping history in mind, I am currently much more concerned about the future.

THE SEARCH

I'm looking for a river
maybe a bubbling brook
   soothing lake
      or roaring ocean beach
to gather every moment of greatness life can offer

I'm looking to focus
   every lesson I've ever learned,
      soaring above the outstretched wings of all feathered friends
who have flown between myself and a full moon

Spectacular dreams ravage my mind,
fueling the raging desire to find a lover,
      an intimate friend
            -maybe both-
surely willing to compromise
            --maybe not-
longing to meet someone capable of sharing on all levels
   the infinite abundance I can envision but not hold,
still determined to capture the entire universe without leaving home
            -No television tonight-
for escape is not the purpose of my journey

Some say I'm looking for too much,
   some say I know not how to look
      some cannot even see me searching
but regardless, I enjoy the comfort of comprehending
   death doesn't matter once you've lived completely,
so, I'm searching to experience what my mind can only conceive
      during splendorous fleeting moments of clarity

Hand on chin, I wonder
   is there a place
maybe a time or perchance
   a someone out there
preparing to cross my path
   who will give echo to such lofty aspirations?

Hopeful passion persists
as my nightly prayer resonates in humble chant,
   "I'm searching and I'll never give up"

BACKSTORY
The Search

We have always held the hope, the belief, the conviction
that there is a better life, a better world, beyond the horizon.
—Franklin D. Roosevelt

Dreams are the seedlings of reality...our only limitations
are those we set up in our own minds.
—Napoleon Hill

They are never alone who are accompanied by noble thoughts.
—Philip Sydney

Paris is universally hailed as one of the most romantic cities on earth. If you are with someone you love, this is most definitely true. However, if you are alone and don't know how to speak French, it can be quite a lonely place.

Such was the case for me when in Paris for a few days after working at a festival in Copenhagen. I spent a fascinating day seeing the sights of Paris, ate dinner at an outdoor café on the Champs-Élysées, and then returned to my hotel room. Staring through my hotel window at the spectacular city lights, I began pondering my place in the world as well as my passionate desire to find love and fulfillment in life.

Looking back at that seminal time, I am pleased to rediscover the burning passion to prevail in my search, a passion that propelled me to ultimately find what I was looking for. My path wasn't easy and was never clearly marked, but The Search officially commemorates the launching of my quest to create the life I wanted to live.

Shortly after writing this poem, I returned to the United States and revamped the focus of my career and romantic life based on the steely commitment of never giving up on dreams for a better existence. In retrospect, this was the beginning of my maturation as I began to focus on creating relationships rather than bouncing from one novel experience to the next. Hopefully this poem will serve as impetus and support for others to persist in their own profound searches.

LOST HISTORY

I'm not old, but I'm aging without love

That's why I like it when you eat off my plate,
it makes me feel connected, young again
to restart my lost history
only friends from the past have shared

If we eat the same
shouldn't we grow the same
feel the same
look the same,
like a master and dog of many years?

So please borrow something
and take my advantage
even if you don't care,
since I need to give and believe in something
whether or not it exists

BACKSTORY
Lost History

People, like facts, do not do well in isolation. Lost History cries out to be replaced by *"shared history"* because shared history creates meaningful emotional bonds. This poem conveys a feeling that accompanied my life for six years while touring as a solo entertainer. I understood how the lonely person depicted in this poem could accept the illusion of an emotional bond just to share some human contact. As a solo entertainer bouncing from city to city on a daily basis, audiences and acquaintances whirled around me in a sea of changing landscapes. It felt as if I was on a high-speed carousel, and everyone else was waving from the perimeter. The only time the proverbial treadmill slowed down was when I returned home, but those returns were usually too brief to connect with old friends who always assumed I was out of town.

In retrospect, those years of my history are fundamentally lost because none of the people I shared them with were a part of my ongoing life. A burning hunger for deeper and more stable relationships was the reason I decided to stop touring and settle down. This poem salutes the importance of faith and connection, two marvelous companions for anyone struggling to transcend a state of lost history. Faith and connection form a solid foundation, fortifying inner strength and perseverance during life's most challenging periods.

I must confess I do like to share plates of food with someone I love. Such activity creates a very comfortable existential feeling of connectedness. My wife and I often order slices of pizza cut down the middle so we can share them. This is one of the growing number of great small pleasures in my life enabled by love, all part of an increasing awareness of the deeply rooted human need to give and share in all phases of life.

In the midst of all this seriousness, I felt compelled to mention the theory that love halts or slows the aging process—a concept always lurking in my mind along with the quirky truth that people and their dogs often grow to look alike.

THE SPECIALIST

More than a hobby, it was a compulsion.
He had to know everything
about something
nobody knew anything about

Sounds crazy,
but soon as anyone else stumbled upon that something
he knew everything about,
he taught them all the details
then would have nothing to do with it,
preferring to brood for weeks on end in his favorite chair
while puffing his favorite pipe

Those were the times his dog was happiest
and all his houseplants flourished,
until the next mixmaster of a day
when this wondrous old man conjured up something new
nobody knew anything about,
methodically emptying his pipe
to grow twenty years younger in an instant
as purpose rejuvenated his soul

In such a cozy world sparkling with inspiration,
each moment swirls with expectations of discovery.
Crystal clear days of thought obey no clock
so the old man repeats his process,
transforming another nothing into a spectacular gem
through the brilliant labor of love
only true genius can bestow

In time,
his new invention is discovered by others
who abuse its divine gift,
never understanding why once again
the specialist abandons his creation

BACKSTORY
The Specialist

When I learn something new, and it happens every day,
I feel a little more at home in the universe.
—Bill Moyers

Men and women like The Specialist are a rare breed. They live and work in seclusion, rarely exposing their lives to the masses. In the corporate world, they are often tucked away in top-secret laboratories. To find such people, one must either do an extensive investigation, or have the good fortune to stumble upon their shrouded paths.

I feel like I know The Specialist. While I do not share his perspective as described in this poem, imagining the brilliance such a mercurial man possesses sparks my curiosity, as there certainly are people in the world who function like he does. I picture a reclusive Leonardo da Vinci type of elderly gentleman completely consumed with his latest passionate creation. He spends endless hours in a studio strewn with piles of diverse paraphernalia only he can comprehend. I ponder what it feels like to be so brilliant, so fierce, yet so alone because of a willingness to completely shut out the world when concocting something uniquely original. I hunger to ask this man a multitude of questions about every dimension of his creative process, hoping to absorb some stellar brilliance while simultaneously avoiding the isolation he has imposed on himself. A part of me wants to be him, but then again, his apparently unbalanced life appears emotionally dangerous.

On its core level, The Specialist is about purity vs. the commercialization of art. It is about mastery of a craft, and mastery is one of man's closest contacts with the divine. A true artist derives his or her greatest pleasure from creating–not selling or marketing each creation. Painters, sculptors, writers, scientists, inventors, musicians all pour their souls into projects of passion. While some become celebrities by steering careers in more commercial directions, those deeply committed to mastering their craft take minimal interest in activities peripheral to the actual work. Commercial success, although alluring, is rarely pursued by a purist.

The Specialist's devotion to his creative process causes him to loathe the dilution of precious work brought on by commercialism. He is a total purist, which explains why he divorces himself from his creations once they become popular. In the final analysis, The Specialist epitomizes purity, an essential quality of great beauty.

WRITER'S BLOCK

Soak my parched tongue with lemon
    and douse this flaming pen
with hydrants of reality
    lest I drift further
into the infinite space
    of unconnected thought

Madness crosses a threshold
    drowning wasted genius
        at lake's bottom
next to rusted beer cans
    and waterlogged shoes

How many times
    can blunted inspiration
        get out of bed,
exhausted from paths leading nowhere,
    before deciding to burn notebooks
stuffed with ideas never to be hatched,
    a lifetime of hopes and dreams
        turned nightmare
by the tyranny of frustration

Prayers give way to desperation
    until a flickering cerebral ember
reignites flames of pulsing creativity
    propelling manic joy
toward another mission
    without end
    without beginning
    without a map
    without hope of ever escaping
each lonely page

BACKSTORY
Writer's Block

The inspiration for Writer's Block came indirectly from the creation of The Specialist. In a manner similar to craving a complete nuclear family, this poem seemed to need a sibling, which inspired the question:

"What would it feel like to be The Specialist on a bad day between projects, with no clear direction in sight?"

For me, such a condition mirrors severe writer's block.

Writer's Block explores the alien thought process of being forced to write a poem without an inciting incident. This process is described as alien because I never start writing a poem under the pressure of such a cold start. In the case of Writer's Block, I simply forced myself to become frustrated and see what jumbled assortment of feelings might materialize.

This exercise provided dynamic insight into the whimsical nature of creative process. Such is the plight of a fleeting creative idea. I have personally endured the great loss of significant breakthroughs hatched while resting in bed. If I didn't rise to write them down immediately, they were always lost by morning. As a result, I have spent many frustrating days searching for the artifacts of a creative flash that moved somewhere within, lost in the synapses of my brain. There are also days of sheer joy when I miraculously recall the tantalizing innovation temporarily lost in those intricate webs of my mind. The synchronistic recall of such gems truly causes a physical sensation, as I can literally feel my mind bend.

Where such sparks come from and how they can be kindled and nurtured is key to accessing the creative mother lode we all possess. Opening to the process is the first step for anyone brave enough to venture into this great sea of unknown delights and pitfalls. I am always cognizant of circling birds of prey, whether I am flying above them or collapsed on the ground as their next target. In a strange way, these birds of prey feel like friends, challenging me to expand my peripheral vision whenever the urge to leap into an idea sucks me in.

As soon as I finished writing Writer's Block, the words for Flash of Genius came to mind, thus completing a chaotic trilogy attempting to demonstrate the profound truth:

"It is often necessary to crawl through the depths of creative despair to reach the immense joy of a flash of genius."

FLASH OF GENIUS

Soaring above clouds
or swept under a rug,
the creative life
knows no middle road

Drinking the mind daily,
a cocktail of ideas
magically combine
to form an elixir
rich DNA sequence
feast for the world

Only in rare moments of clarity
exists the possibility
to create a masterpiece.
Miss your moment
and a lifetime may pass
before the next

A life so lived
breathes tomorrow's air today
preparing for the next
precious
elusive
flash of genius

BACKSTORY
Flash Of Genius

The most beautiful thing we can experience is the mysterious.
It is the source of all true art and science.
—Albert Einstein

Be open to epiphanies, sudden realizations of significant truths,
usually arising out of commonplace events.
Such moments can determine the course of your life.
—Robert U. Akeret

Flashes of genius are what I live for. I've had a few in my life and missed a few as well. This poem is dedicated to the rare, apocalyptic flashes capable of causing momentous change. Although such flashes of creativity touch down like tornadoes, they are not quite as unpredictable as many people assume. There are numerous ways to cultivate creative surges.

In my opinion, the most important ingredient in cultivating inner creativity is freedom, meaning freedom of the mind to travel wherever it wants to go without encumbrance. Once a creative seed is planted, directing the mind toward a specific direction and/or subject is extremely helpful. At this point, the mind secretly begins churning on its new subject, but like a slot machine, finds no schedule for achieving the jackpot of an intoxicating creative flash.

Another essential ingredient of preparation is readiness. In this instance, readiness means having a notebook or dictating device handy at all times. I have learned that actively remembering components of a creative flash prevents the flash from expanding in my mind because my brain wastes valuable mental energy straining to retain the initial thought. Having slept through a few major flashes, I can confirm that once a creative flash is gone, it rarely returns, leaving a hollow feeling similar to bereavement. Consequently, the warning of this poem is:

Nurture your flashes!

Living a creative life, while potentially thrilling, is also quite precarious. It is the only life I can conceive of living, no matter what the consequences. For those who choose to embark on such a journey, tighten the chinstrap on your crash helmet, and to quote Star Wars:

"May the force be with you."

…since any moment of existence can bring a once-in-a-lifetime meteor shower of inspired ideas destined to change your life forever.

MODERN QUESTION

It seems
I never get what I want
when I want so much
that it hurts

So I learn not to want
what I want
since I only get
what I get
no matter what I want,
more happily accepting
what is
is what should be

To want, or not to want?
That is the modern question
—Whether 'tis nobler all things unfurl
   as they should
without regard to desire
by divine plan
    or not,
may the gift of
  what is
replace the heavily burdened
  what we want to be
in a weightless joy
that satisfies all hunger
  wanting not to want
inhaling every moment
   at peace with itself

BACKSTORY
Modern Question

Modern Question reflects a sentiment similar to the next poem in this book, Tree of More. While both poems explore the human propensity to want, they are written in very different styles. The condition of wanting is so universal in every aspect of life that it cannot be avoided. Unfortunately, wanting is also a great source of suffering, as so many wants go unfulfilled.

I have wrestled with the many sides of desire in all its forms and have concluded, although it is impossible to eliminate desire, it is possible to minimize wanting and thereby avoid craving. Unfullfilled desire is what dreams are for. Experience has taught me to replace wanting with gratitude and acceptance of *"what is"*. Minimizing the urge to want maximizes levels of inner peace. It converts life's special gifts into pleasant surprises.

A word I have attempted to eliminate from my vocabulary is *"should"*. Having observed many people fail to mold their world into what they think it should be, I have come to realize that accepting the world as it is produces much better outcomes. When transcribing Modern Question from the hotel stationery it was originally written on, I found the following note in the bottom corner of the page:

> *These days,*
> *It takes*
> *So much more*
> *To have it all*

TREE OF MORE

The more I know
the less I say,
The less I say
the more it means,
The more it means
the less I say
The more I give
the more I have

The more I have
the less I need,
The less I need
the freer I am,
The freer I am
the more I love
The more I love
the more I receive
The more I receive
the more I give
The more I give
the more I have

And round it goes,
The more I learn
the more I seek
The more I seek
the more I know
The more I know
the more I give
The more I give
the more I have

Teaching me
To give is to have
To love is to learn
To need less is to have more
As giving more
leads to abundant silent riches
woven into the fabric of life

BACKSTORY
Tree Of More

I have the greatest of all riches: That of not desiring them.
—Eleonora Duse

Poor is not the person who has too little, but the person who craves more.
—Lucius Annaeus Seneca (first century AD)

I make myself rich by making my wants few.
—Henry David Thoreau

Tree of More is a stylistic step out of my comfort zone planned as an exercise in simplicity. This poem's seminal goal was to explore the relationship between *less* and *more*. Rather than search for expansive images, I chose repetition to reinforce intended meaning. Rather than open a door for broad interpretation, I hammered repeatedly on similar nails, hoping to clarify fundamental concepts by vertically piling up thoughts.

Envisioning myself a courtroom lawyer methodically building his case, I stacked up basic beliefs to resemble the trunk of a tree. Supported by its base, Tree of More blossoms through its upper limbs, an image intended as metaphor for the ongoing development of our lives. Even though I know the lines of this poem by heart, I still sometimes get tripped up when reading it to others. It presents an endless challenge to read phrases in correct cadence so each line builds on the one before. The rationale for Tree of More is derived from three realizations:

-*Givers receive immense invisible gifts from their generosity.*
-*Wisdom frequently sits in silence waiting for someone to ask the right question.*
-*Freedom is an essential human need touching every dimension of life.*

Continuing this line of thinking led me to the conclusion that in love,

the greatest freedom is the freedom to stay forever,

which crystallized a broader vision of all opposites being connected by divine threads, the same way leaves attach to trees.

SHOPPING CART

My shopping cart learned to read
and now it can't believe
what it sees

Labels on cases of paper towels
proclaim 8 rolls equals 12
while other cases brag 12 rolls equals 18.
Signs in the meat aisle
say pork is the new white meat
while clothing billboards
declare gray is the new black

As my shopping cart wobbles through
overstocked supermarket aisles
it counts rolls of paper towels
while reading signs that claim
    up is the new down
    fantasy is the new reality
    anxiety is the new happiness
    lies are the new truth
    Earth is the new Mars
life is dying
progress is a disaster
and unless love replaces hate
    the end is near

BACKSTORY
Shopping Cart

On the way to a local supermarket, I read a Kenneth Cole billboard proclaiming gray is the new black, which reminded me of the television commercial declaring pork to be the new white meat. These proclamations almost prepared me for a very existential shopping experience at the local Stop & Shop.

The paper towel aisle was brimming with complicated special offers in which the volume of each package needed a computer to be calculated. By varying the number of sheets on a roll, each case of paper towels claimed to be more rolls than it actually was.

The numbers mentioned in this poem were copied directly from wrapper labels on the cases of paper towels I purchased that day. I wasn't sure how many rolls I actually owned at the end of my shopping adventure, so I consulted with my shopping cart to see if it could clear up the confusion.

As this poem demonstrates, my shopping cart's answer was much more profound than expected.

WHILE YOU SLEEP

While you sleep
I rest in silence with one ear open
    to the lovely sounds you make
and thrill to your deep breaths,
for they tell me you are relaxed
    at home in my bed
as I pray for the depth and ultimate comfort of your sleep
while maintaining my motionless vigil,
fearful you will awaken to discover
    I am a spy

While you sleep
I delight at the smacking of your lips
    your snorts and sighs
while I silently chuckle at the gurgles
of your stomach—that miniature factory
starting the production of your loveliness

You wonder why
I treasure such sleepless nights
because you cannot see yourself in your finest hours,
    so soft and vulnerable,
a delight to touch
yet so distant in your heavenly dreams
I dare not move in your direction
except with my ears

While you sleep
I am busy absorbing
the splendor of what it means
to be with someone as a way of life

We even share the same toothbrush now,
and sometimes I wonder
what you have to say
about the times
you rest in silence
while I sleep

BACKSTORY
While You Sleep

At first, I was afraid to show While You Sleep to my wife. I was afraid she would develop insomnia from the fear I was studying her every night. When I finally got up the courage to show her this poem, she smiled and admitted she had done her own bit of spying as well. This was a great relief and gave me the insight such spying is only natural when you are sleeping next to a great treasure. A protective instinct takes hold in addition to the pure joy of being connected to someone so lovely.

If While You Sleep is the way you feel about your lover, the only greater pleasure is to find out your lover treasures you in the same way.

MY LOVE

For every step you take
may you see
the bed of roses
I lay at your feet
as the petals of my love
peel away all resistance
allowing you to touch
my throbbing heart
that beats only for you

THE ARCHAEOLOGIST

When I was nine years old,
my father took me on an expedition.
Well, it was merely a fossil park
    within shouting distance of Niagara Falls

As soon as the park's curator
outfitted us with two shiny hammers,
a primordial excitement sprang up inside me.
Breathless as a coffee-drinking Labrador on choke collar,
I dragged my father toward the park's barren field
    to search for buried dinosaurs

After hours of chipping away at mounds of unconcerned rock,
I finally managed to unearth the petrified remains of a tiny snail.
    Surely this snail was once eaten by a dinosaur!
Discoveries of such magnitude
greatly intensify a directionless search
so, while a misty rain drenched my weary father
    who I now believe
was dreaming of a warm bowl of chowder,
    my passionate pursuit of antiquity's secrets hammered on

Fifty years later, I recall this soggy day
while embarking on a new expedition,
this time as spiritual archaeologist
    excavating fossil remains of early family life
as if dinosaurs once roamed within

The internal debate rages daily:
    Am I courageous, or merely digging too deep?
While rummaging through foggy memories
resembling the trail of a petrified snail,
will I harm the fragile house of my mind
    or unearth new truths
destined to enlighten my delicate psyche?

Truth is dangerous when presented without perspective.
People drown in riptides of reality,
unable to discern where fiction began in their lives.
My father died without uttering an introspective word,
in fact
the whole family tree perished without a clue
    leaving no tools to unearth bewildering secrets
time has covered with dust

Is emotional evolution susceptible to carbon dating,
    or do I know more about some petrified snail's journey
        through the belly of a never-found Niagara Falls dinosaur
than I know about myself?

So I dig,
then I dig some more,
always curious about secret digging done by others
wondering whether excavation is the answer
    or merely an extinct remnant
buried deep within our imagination

BACKSTORY
The Archaeologist

If you look deeply into the palm of your hand,
you will see your parents and all generations of your ancestors.
All of them are alive in this moment. Each is present in your body.
You are the continuation of each of these people.
—Thich Nhat Hanh

When I was nine years old, my parents took me to Niagara Falls. On our first day there, we experienced the wondrous power of The Falls by trekking across a rickety wooden footbridge dangerously close to the endless torrents of water cascading in all directions. I remember being outfitted with full-length yellow rain slickers and matching floppy yellow hats. We looked like salty fishermen.

As we held on tightly to the railing along a creaky path of wooden slats, blinding spray roared up from all directions. We were soaked from head to toe, and thrilled by every drop. The next morning, my mother read in her tourist pamphlet about a fossil park on the Canadian side of Niagara Falls.
I immediately began begging to be taken there, as dinosaurs had fascinated me since the day I was born. Dinosaurs never scared me. Rather, they seemed like childhood friends I must have played with in a previous lifetime.

Since inclement weather caused our scheduled activity to be cancelled, my mom suggested to my dad that a trip to the fossil park was perfect for father and son, so dad got the lucky assignment of accompanying me on my first archaeological dig. Little did I know, it would also be my last.

The highlight of this most unglamorous dig was the unearthing of a fossilized snail. This electrifying discovery convinced me further digging would reveal an actual dinosaur carcass, so I persistently hammered away at endless bland rock formations while my father stood paternally by my side. In my mind's eye, I can still picture a cold, drizzly rain soaking us the whole afternoon. Finally, a fossil park ranger tracked us down to announce the park was closing. That was probably the high point of my father's afternoon. In retrospect, I feel badly my father had to spend one of his treasured vacation days watching me hammer for dead snails.

The Archaeologist was written after all my family elders died. Their extinction from my world paralleled the prehistoric disappearance of dinosaurs, as so many family questions remained unanswered. Wallowing in the mystery of my genealogy ignited a deep yearning to better understand the human psyche, a subject that eventually replaced my original passion for archaeology.

FATHER'S DAY ON CHRISTMAS

Tiny infant fingers
pull ribbons from boxes
as a teething mouth
drools over toys,
not noticing hair grow between the knuckles
    until years later
a deeper voice
asks the barber for a shave

Who else would have given me
his eyes
his jaw
his powerful hands
and off-beat ways,
not to mention a hairy chest?

It was my genetic Santa Claus,
    Dad
delivering life's hereditary toolbox.
Thanks for leaving me your sunglasses
that see gold in junkyards
and makes mouths full of lemon smile

I savor sweet father memories
like classic movies,
but despite an endless craving,
    these reruns
only survive in my mind

Each time Dad visits in a dream
my innards cringe with secret sobs
realizing he had to leave forever,
much too soon after giving out the presents

BACKSTORY
Father's Day On Christmas

The night my father died from a sudden heart attack, I was soundly sleeping in my Ann Arbor, Michigan apartment. The phone rang at 3am and my mother's sister instructed me to come home immediately. The next morning, I took the first flight available and arrived to a very grim scene featuring my mother sitting motionless in a large club chair. She was dressed in black, with black nail polish on her trembling fingers. The blinds were drawn shut and a dreary silence haunted the crowded room of red-eyed relatives.

To fully appreciate this morbid scene, one must be given some insight into the dynamic nature of my extremely vibrant parents. They exuded cheerfulness in every instant of life, and my mother had never worn anything black in her life. She was always awash in color, which blended perfectly with her sunny disposition. Witnessing this living room scene, I instantly ran to my mother's side, and for the next few years spent every available moment creating ways to help her combat overwhelming grief.

Father's Day on Christmas was written a week before Christmas, two years after my father's funeral. The scene of ignition for this poem was an airplane at 35,000 feet. At that time I was a touring entertainer en route to perform a show in Wisconsin. Usually I did not talk with strangers when flying, but on this occasion became immersed in conversation with the woman next to me. Somehow the recent passing of my father surfaced, causing me to describe the scenario in my mother's apartment the morning after my father's death. My conversation partner commented on the great loss I had suffered in losing my father. This comment flabbergasted me, as I had never stopped to consider the death of my father as **my** loss. It had always seemed to be exclusively my **mother's** loss. No family member, friend or acquaintance had ever even mentioned this event as **my** personal loss. Instead, everyone had always complimented me on taking such good care of my bereaved mother. This revelation left me reeling. I must have turned white as a sheet, because the woman asked me if I was OK.
I nodded *"Yes"* and then excused myself.

Fortunately, the plane was not full, so I was able to scurry to the back of the aircraft and sit in an empty row. After catching my breath, I took out a sheet of paper, as the urge to write overcame me. Father's Day on Christmas came out in a manner that parallels throwing up. Unfamiliar emotions swelled up from my chest and words heaved themselves onto the sheet of paper with a mind of their own. As I finished writing, I began to sob. It must have been louder than I realized, because a stewardess rushed over to ask me if anything was wrong. Through my tears, which were truly tears of relief I muttered, *"I'm fine."*
She noticed I had written something and asked what it was, so I told her it was a poem about my recently deceased father.

The stewardess was immediately drawn into my emotional field as she informed me her father had died very recently. I offered her my poem, and she read it. Within moments, both of us were sobbing together.

DISSERTATION ON THE EXISTENCE OF MOLTEN SNOW

Molten snow exists as an illusory paradox
to tease the imagination,
dissolving itself by definition
into steamy cauldrons slowly poured over words,
scalding the eyes with fiery-hot liquid
before a sizzling indecipherable steam
rises skyward

Close your eyes and picture molten snow
  —It is impossible to conjure clearly—
Is it scalding-hot snowflakes, or glowing volcanic lava?
Is it steamy slush or toxic gas?
Can it possibly exist, or is it nature's only impossibility?

The eclectic value of molten snow
is akin to poetic license,
as artistically crafted words
explode contradictory images that sail weightlessly across a page
from and to nowhere
except somehow invisible particles of ethereal communication
are magically conveyed between distant minds
now profoundly connected by invisible threads of thought

BACKSTORY
Dissertation On The Existence Of Molten Snow

The capacity to embrace paradox—to perceive the validity of opposites,
is a major key to wisdom.
—M. Scott Peck

The phrase Molten Snow drifted into my consciousness one summer afternoon while in Lake Placid, NY. The temperature was 86 degrees and I was standing outside the Olympic ice skating arena. Piled up in front of me was a huge mound of snow more than ten feet high, the residual scrapings from continual cleanings of the massive adjacent indoor skating rink. My friends and I proceeded to engage in a spirited snowball fight while dressed in bathing suits, and then we went swimming.

This incongruous mound of snow piled up on a summer's day conjured up the image of molten snow in my mind. I tried to picture what molten snow might look like, but could not. My logical mind kept insisting molten snow is just hot water, but my poetic mind wouldn't let go of the dramatic desire to commemorate this newly created phrase. An internal argument persisted the entire afternoon while I swam in the lake, and it raged on as I tried to sleep that night. In the middle of the night I turned on the light in my hotel room and grabbed a piece of hotel stationery. The result was this poem.

Every time I read Molten Snow, the same cerebral argument revives itself. I begin wrestling with visions of what molten snow looks like, and whether or not it would burn someone who touched it. Underlying this vision is the essence of poetic license, since the contradiction inherent in molten snow provides fertile ground for poetic expression. This exemplifies the beauty of language—its ability to describe the indescribable and convey images from one mind to another. Once we apply our imagination to language, there are no limits to what we can construct.

That is the true meaning of Molten Snow.

GET WELL NOTE

People come and go
like the tides
but no one forgets
the brightest sunset
on their favorite beach

So it is with me
coming and going daily
wherever I am
carries the brightness of your smile,
making thoughts of your recovery
part of my day
and I hope
this note
aids in the mending

BACKSTORY
Get Well Note

A number of years ago, I worked at the Variety Arts Center in Los Angeles as a talent coordinator. Every day, at the entrance of the beautiful theatre club entry foyer, a lovely woman named Ellie cheerfully greeted me from behind a rather dramatic elevated podium. She greeted everyone with a warm smile and was always in a good mood. Ellie was a regal yet humble woman, probably in her mid sixties. She was a fixture at her lobby perch for years, adding a lovely touch to the arts center with her sweet, maternal demeanor. She always knew where everyone was and what everyone was doing, thereby serving as the hub of the entire venue.

Ellie and I became friends. Before going up to my office, I always chatted with her. She took interest in hearing about my life outside of work, often telling me about her children and extended family. One day, as I made my entrance into the building, I noticed Ellie wasn't on her usual perch. A man was sitting in her place, and he was not smiling.

When I asked where Ellie was, the man became teary and almost started to cry. He told me the bad news—Ellie was in the hospital. The night before, Ellie and her husband had been driving on the highway when their car developed a flat tire. Her husband managed to steer their car safely to the side of the road where they stood on the shoulder, waiting for roadside assistance. Unfortunately, a truck swerved onto the shoulder and hit Ellie. She was very seriously injured and would not be returning to work for a long time, if ever. Devastated by this news, I solemnly trudged up to my office in a fog. The question in my mind was,

"What could I possibly do for this wonderful person who was now in such a dreadful situation?"

Ellie was in no condition to receive visitors, so I mailed a Get Well Note to her hospital room. For the rest of my time at the Variety Arts Center, I checked on Ellie's recovery every day. The news was always tentative at best. Ellie survived her hospital stay, but did not return to work. I never saw her again after her tragic accident, but she has often been in my thoughts.

Every time I read this poem, it stirs up my original wish that somehow my words were of some benefit to Ellie in her time of great duress. The passage of time has given Get Well Note a more universal feeling, hopefully applicable for any loved one who is suffering.

CEMENT

Cement is like mud
that got frozen.
Cement is an optimist
who never smiles.
Mix it downhill like a martini
    then get out of its way

Cement is always in style.
Some people wear it for shoes
when taking a swim
-that way one pair lasts a lifetime

Don't ignore cement.
Someday you might fall on it
    and get hurt

Never insult cement
because cement never forgets.
It doesn't have to remember
    or remind you
if it's written in cement
    then it is forever

BACKSTORY
Cement

You are probably wondering, how could Cement possibly have a backstory? Well, it does, and it's a bit quirky. The story began one afternoon in New York City. A stonemason was repairing the sidewalk in front of our apartment building, and being a curious person, I started asking him questions about how to mix cement properly.

Somewhere in the middle of our conversation, the mason asked me what I did for a living. I told him I was in the entertainment business, but also wrote poetry. Displaying a spark of sarcastic wit, the mason quipped,

"I guarantee you will never write a poem about cement!"

We both had a good laugh about his comment, but I immediately stored away the challenge he had just presented. As soon as we were done talking, I charged up to my apartment and grabbed pen and paper. Then I stormed down the steps and raced out to one of my favorite writing spots in a local park, where Cement poured out of me.

By the time I returned home, the mason had already finished his repair. I never saw him again, so I could never show him the poem he inspired.

Hopefully, someone will buy him this book for Christmas!

NO HEADLINES

On the golf course daffodils begin to bloom.
My neighbor mows his lawn while two snails fall in love.
A bus collides with a truck
    as new wars break out for no reason.
It is winter below the equator

A huge gorilla yawns mightily,
    delighting everyone at the zoo.
More adventurers climb Mount Everest
    but can't get back down.
An old man plays his clarinet in the street
    urging his city to become a community.
From her rocker, Grandmother hears the old man's clarinet
        and begins to cry.
She mourns her dead husband,
wondering how it all passed by so quickly

The gorilla yawns again and gets a banana
…the snails file for divorce,
the truck driver gets out of the hospital
    and hires a lawyer.
It is summer below the equator

The old man sells his clarinet to pay for dinner
    just before Grandma's phone rings.
She dusts it off in time to hear her grandson sing
        "Happy Birthday"
Now her tears wear a smile,
    as war rages on
this time on a different continent

The truck driver wins his case and becomes a millionaire.
It's all in the newspaper my dog brings to our breakfast table
    in return for a pat on his head.
He licks my hand, then checks his hairdo in the hallway mirror.
It is spring below the equator

Greenland's iceberg thaws with a groan.
My love serves some eggs, then smiles in my direction
    reading me like an encyclopedia.
I return her smile and throw away the newspaper
since nothing has changed in the last thousand years

BACKSTORY
No Headlines

A good newspaper is a nation talking to itself.
—Arthur Miller

No Headlines was written after a stroll on a golf course. I don't play golf, but love walking on golf courses when nobody is playing. One sunny day in early spring, I took an afternoon stroll on the back nine of a nearby course. The 18th hole ended at a sparkling row of fully-bloomed daffodils. I would like to officially thank those daffodils for inspiring me to write No Headlines. It marks my first attempt to piece together fictitious events in a stream-of-consciousness.

No Headlines' trajectory highlights mankind's need to focus on universal truths instead of isolated events. My challenge was to utilize multiple incongruous events to create an eclectic montage from which meaning could be extracted. Stringing together a trail of seemingly random events and time frames, No Headlines hops its way home with the toss of a newspaper, discarding the latest news from a world in which even family dogs have been infected with the affliction of vanity.

Somehow, this rollercoaster ride led me back home to a point of resolution, as mixing the absurd with the mundane conjured up memories of studying the eclectic theatrical plays of Ionesco. Such mixtures are analogous to volatile chemical experiments capable of yielding unexpected combustible results.

I could easily go overboard with a detailed analysis of this poem's evolution, but let it suffice to say No Headlines is one of my favorites.

CHANGES

No loss
is suffered
without some gain
though loss
often drowns itself in self-pity

No gain is achieved
without some loss,
such loss often overlooked
in celebration or complacency

So continues
the unblemished paradox of progress
perpetually destined
to re-create the primitive

History's guarantee,
despite the infinite changes
    of modern times
assures us
everything will once again
be the same

BACKSTORY
Changes

We must be the change we wish to see in the world.
—Mahatma Gandhi

The best way to predict the future is to invent it.
—Allen Curtis Kay

Changes was the last backstory I wrote. Once all the backstories were completed, it was time to order the poems. This proved more challenging than expected. During this organizational process, I began to observe similarities and differences between various entries.

Changes emerged as a close relative of No Headlines. Both arrive at similar conclusions after taking different paths to their common destination. Changes was written during a period of reflection while I recuperated from a painful injury. My mood was much more playful when writing No Headlines, which began as an experiment in style. Changes arose from firsthand experience that pain truly is a great teacher, and the greatest tragedy is to suffer pain without learning its lesson. Most of the significant shifts in my life have been launched by painful experiences that forced me to reconsider my goals and change direction. The fortunate paradox is, painful experiences can potentially give birth to great happiness and/or success. Conversely, all triumphs contain potential seeds of destruction. Changes laments an unfortunate truth:

Despite creating what is interpreted as progress,
mankind still remains primitive in many underlying ways.

By not heeding lessons of history, our species seems destined to periodically regress to its primitive roots. This creates a vicious historical cycle reminding us current human emotional and spiritual dispositions still greatly resemble our ancient ancestors. Until our collective consciousness catches up with technology, humanity is constantly at great risk of destroying itself.

COLUMBUS WAS HERE

How does one discover something that is already there,
               or invent a beach?
…and who decides what is beautiful
        in this bumper sticker of a world?
A dollar isn't worth a dime in the woods,
        and what do you call a musician without his instrument?

Doesn't it make you curious
        which dinosaur stepped on the first clock,
               and who was foolish enough to rent planet Earth
                       to humans?

Meanwhile, be proud of your dandruff
        and don't worry about a thing,
just realize time has repossessed your mind,
        history does repeat itself,
               and only fools make the same mistake twice
unless they destroy the future
                       their first time around

BACKSTORY
Columbus Was Here

Columbus Was Here symbolizes a rebellious period I experienced many years ago. I started writing it with a growl on my face and finished with a smile. Sparked by a national controversy over whether or not Columbus was the first explorer to discover America, the edginess in this rant contains a number of my pet peeves at the time. Primarily, I was annoyed so much fuss was made about what explorer landed in New York first. I couldn't see the value in arguing over this detail five hundred years after the fact, when it was impossible to prove any claim. Whether or not Eric the Red ever made it down to the New York area didn't seem important when our current world had so many other pressing problems to solve. Besides, everyone had already gotten used to taking a day off from work on Columbus Day.

The reference to dandruff was a sarcastic attempt to poke fun at television commercials that constantly tell us about what is wrong with ourselves so we will buy their products. Columbus Was Here is essentially a series of graffiti phrases depicting the contradictions inherent in modern American life. I envision it thriving on the brick wall of a deserted building.

CUSTER'S NEW LAST STAND

While life rages on
    across our besieged planet
people with hidden agendas
continually attempt to revise history
hoping to improve the future
    by changing the past

My son's textbook
    now tells him
Custer was a restaurateur
serving free chowder to Indians
    as if he were a charitable foundation

This textbook
recalls one frigid evening
under a North Dakota sky
when soup was served lukewarm
infuriating Custer's Native American friends
    to the point of violence,
hence a battle ensued
and the saintly Custer was slain
along with his brave friends,
    all heroes drowned in bowls of cold soup

Such a story appears nonsense
    until accepted as fact
by young impressionable minds
    reading schoolbooks

This exaggerated example
demonstrates what can happen
when the past is reconstructed
from various points of view
    all biased
and wrestling to achieve dominance
over the veracity of facts
which have no loyalty
    to any cause

BACKSTORY
Custer's New Last Stand

There are no facts, only interpretations.
—Friedrich Nietzsche

Most of the trouble in the world is caused by people wanting to be important.
—T.S. Eliot

Custer's New Last Stand was inspired by a news report announcing certain states in America plan to revise their history books in an attempt to inject various new interpretations of our nation's historical events. Any move toward altering the basis of our origins strikes me as treacherous. Revisionist history creates the possibility of destabilizing our view of the past, which is the foundation we all stand on.

Applying any form of ideology to historical events opens the door to all sorts of misrepresentations, putting our historical roots in jeopardy of becoming mangled. To demonstrate my disdain for such a practice, it seemed appropriate to create an example of how distorted history can become when restated from the wrong perspective. The truth is I know little about the inner psyche of General Custer or his adversaries on that fateful day. It is highly doubtful cold soup had anything to do with Custer's predicament.

The central issue of Custer's Last Stand is the fact that others who also know little about this event could be swayed into believing any ridiculous story printed in a textbook. Modern society is already battling daily mounds of misinformation flowing through the internet. The minds of young students are easily impressionable, so it is absolutely essential our history be carefully researched and documented by a broad spectrum of scholars devoid of ideological agendas.

Society's mandatory goal must be to tell our history accurately and fully so we learn the lessons of history. If facts and stories are distorted by factions with differing agendas, then our history, and subsequently our future, risk becoming a muddled mess.

AWAITING MY CALL

So powerful is your magnet,
    my orbit
follows as servant
even when you are away

So dwarfed and puny I feel
so helpless to scale your foreboding cliff,
I wallow in the valley of low tide
bleeding from pecks of hungry vultures
circling my sagging flesh

Like a shrinking warrior
unable to find his reflection in the mirror
afraid to pick up the phone
and grow strong by confessing weakness,
    I vacuum carpets
    punch pillows
    capture insects
in a series of Pyrrhic victories
designed for a loser

Within this isolated suffering
my humble imagination envisions you
joyously conquering all without me.
I hunger for the sound of your voice
only to settle for its echo in my mind
while flashes of your lovely face
dance inside my eyes

How was I to know
while I drowned
in the privacy of my own home,
you were sleepless by your phone
awaiting my call

BACKSTORY
Awaiting My Call

The young man described in this poem is me. I have felt my own insignificance in the eyes of a potential girlfriend, only to be shocked to later find out she was just as enamored with me.

Awaiting My Call is the story of a young man on the cusp of learning how to fight through his insecurities. He just needs to muster some self-confidence, a confidence that will enable his inner strength to develop. In this poem, he is not quite ready to become vulnerable enough to reap the rewards of love, choosing to allow other activities get in the way. We can only hope the pain of not getting the girl of his dreams will eventually lead this young man to develop a warrior spirit in matters of the heart. One of the most valuable lessons I learned about life is the need to embrace any potential harm necessary to overcome obstacles blocking my path.

Overcoming inner fears is often the main obstacle in facing moments of truth. This is true in all aspects of life. If we don't pick up the phone, how do we know who may be awaiting our call? How many opportunities may be out there waiting for us if we simply muster enough courage to take the first step?

SECRET CODE

When all I do is talk
    It's because I don't know what to do
When I talk too much
    It's because I have nothing important to say
When I talk too fast
    It's so you won't know what I feel
When I talk too loud
    It's because I'm afraid you will go away
When I talk too softly
    It's so you'll move in closer
        but when I don't talk at all,
BEWARE!

BACKSTORY
Secret Code

Unfortunately, people do not come with instructions or warranties.
I wrote Secret Code for a girlfriend who complained she just couldn't figure me
out. The next day, I decided to give her some insight about how to interpret my
behavior.

While this poem did not solve the significant issues at the root of our rocky
relationship, it did clarify a few truths about my personality. It has often come in
handy when explaining myself in subsequent relationships, as it still is accurate
to this day. Judging from the reaction of many people who have read this piece, I
am not alone in the profile described in Secret Code, as the interpretation of my
behavior seems to demonstrate some universal male traits.

ROYALTY

Royalty
 is born
never elected
as if blood
owns privileged vineyards
where the wealthiest grapes
steer all dreams of the multitudes
from within secluded walls of a castle

Into this scenario
the next royal embryo prepares daily
    within mother's royal womb
unaware of his special destiny
until blazing trumpets
announce inherited responsibilities
far beyond most men's mortal reach,
    yet mere child's play
to one of such celebrated lineage
filled with the red satin semen of kings
flowing through his veins

This boy's mind, kidnapped at birth
is groomed cautiously
inside nurturing confines of the royal suite,
until years later, long since being crowned
the child-king rises from a restless sleep
chilled by the realization his throne
has been polluted by past generations of guile
brewed from clandestine secrets
known only to ghosts of deceased ancestors

Enslaved by the great burden of royalty
this courageous young man
unearths his natural self
barely in time to save his kingdom,
finally deciphering where truth
meets the edge of power

BACKSTORY
Royalty

Royalty was inspired by the royal wedding of Prince William to Kate Middleton, and the subsequent birth of their son George. The immense pomp and circumstance surrounding these two events stirred up memories of the complex career of William's father, Prince Charles, which then recalled the incredible rise and demise of Princess Diana. A recent movie served to further inspire this poem—*W.E.*—a film depicting the very dramatic love story of King Edward VIII and Wallace Simpson. King Edward's story is a fascinating tale, as he spent most of his life fighting the weight of royal birth and eventually abdicated his throne to marry the woman he loved.

These stories illustrate how much royal lives are planned even before conception, and how much of a struggle it must be for royal descendants to establish their autonomy or even know themselves. External influences and pressures seem overwhelming for those of royal descent, especially young would-be kings.

The evolution of parliamentary-styled government has reduced current royalty to figurehead status in England, but that is a global anomaly. Ever since the early Egyptian and Roman Empires, lethal machinations of royal courts and bloody wars initiated by kings are well documented. Throughout ancient and modern history, succession of royalty has often occurred suddenly, and many kings were crowned while still in boyhood.

Royalty is an outsider's attempt to morph into the shoes of a young boy who is indoctrinated as king much too early in life, with the daunting ordeal of finding his own true self to become a leader worthy of such a lofty position.

PATH TO A DREAM

Never straight lines
as if butterflies
flitting en route to flowery nectar,
dreams soar through clouds
dive under oceans
detour around mountains
without ever taking an eye off the prize

No cloud too high
no ocean too deep
no mountain too wide,
paths of such journeys
bravely trek through the unfamiliar,
enduring endless challenges
as unrelenting obstacles
constantly entice the coward in us to retreat

It is impossible to ignore
the steely gleam in eyes of warriors
committed to their dreams,
each doggedly stalking a goal
 -that coveted accomplishment worthy of risking it all

Moments of glory need no explanation
for triumph is a language in itself,
all pain quickly forgotten
the instant one finger
finally touches the tip of fulfillment

Salivating over the edge of each passionate dream
we begin to resemble fish
nibbling at an alluring hook
suspended from a magic rod
as we swim the paths of undersea butterflies
darting chaotically in any direction
that seems to offer assistance
        Just reel us in,
    We swallowed the bait long ago
as we digest the hymn of eternal wisdom:
        Pursuing dreams
    Is what makes life worthwhile

BACKSTORY
Path To A Dream

The future belongs to those who believe in the beauty of their dreams.
—Eleanor Roosevelt

Sometimes dreams are wiser than waking.
—Black Elk (Ogla Sioux)

A goal is a dream with a deadline.
—Napoleon Hill

Path To A Dream surfaced while I swam underwater in a swimming pool. The pool was empty, so I was able to swim around without fear of bumping into anyone. Taking advantage of this freedom, I swam chaotically as the butterflies described in this poem. All sorts of ideas, desires, plans and images flowed through my mind's eye. A new phrase quickly got my juices flowing. The phrase was: *"It is better to die for a dream than to live without one."*

Lap after lap, my conscious mind began to notice I was simultaneously immersed in a dream state. This led to the realization I spend much of my life dreaming, regardless of other conscious activities. In fact, most people have dreams floating through their minds on a regular basis. Even when we are awake, dreams continually pass through our minds, attempting to grab attention and be evaluated for deeper consideration. My belief is that dreams are an all-encompassing mental activity everyone constantly engages in. However, the dimensionality of dreams varies greatly from person to person, as does the willingness to embrace these mysterious impulses.

Even though the water in the swimming pool was cool, my brain began to overheat. I hopped out of the water and sprinted toward the nearest pen and paper. My dream state had been converted to reality. As water dripped down from my hair, the words for Path To A Dream poured out. So did this backstory.

This is the only backstory composed at the same time as its companion poem. For some reason, the act of creating Path To A Dream caused me to ponder the nature of dreams and seek clearer parameters for defining them. Not every dream leads to creation of a large corporation, a major invention or the perfect lover suddenly appearing. The genii usually stays in the bottle. Although grandiose dreams grab more attention, large dreams often rest on the shoulders of a conglomeration of many smaller, subtler ones.

Contemplating dreams brought on an uncomfortable feeling of approaching chaos. To restore order, I formulated five major dream categories:

Desires
Creative Ideas
Visions
Action Plans
Redirected Scenarios

This list demonstrates various ways dreams influence desires, visions, ideas, and action plans. An action plan can be as simple as one's dream of how a day might go or as complicated as the major restructuring of a factory. Action plan dreams are not necessarily straightforward predictors of what will transpire. They are often convoluted messes of fantastic possibilities revealing a person's emotional condition combined with external factors surrounding each specific situation. Once activated, all dream categories interact with each other to form a substantial variety of combinations.

For example, desire motivates searches for creative ideas, which can develop into action plans. Compelling visions can stimulate desire, while redirected scenarios often lead to revamped action plans. Redirected Scenarios are a source of fascination to me, as we all replay and revise various memories, especially traumatic ones. I confess to being a huge scenario dreamer. My mind constantly tackles future scenarios from multiple angles to anticipate future challenges and formulate appropriate responses.

Unfortunately, most people unconsciously impose devastating filters that preclude grandiose dreams from hatching and expanding. When someone suppresses a big dream, they unwittingly limit their creativity, general awareness, and potential greatness. To me, this is a tragedy. Even worse, many walk around with dreams of others psychically imbedded in their minds, making it supremely difficult to decipher their life's purpose.

Path To A Dream urges you adopt a warrior spirit toward dreams, sort them out, and follow the paths they illuminate. Dreams contain all our finest qualities along with our deepest fears. The boundless combinations of dreams and paths create a complex labyrinth, as each path to a dream reveals a different outcome, and each dream creates its own unique path. Once we wake up to the power dreams possess, it is time to choose wisely and pursue with passion. If a goal is a dream with a deadline, then dreams are goals without deadlines. This mental outlook takes away some of the time pressure associated with dream fulfillment. My advice is to live as close as possible to your grandest dreams, always keeping them in mind as long-term goals.

That is the most direct route to true destiny.

EULOGY FOR A CRAB

Daily beach walks
    consume themselves
with searches for perfect shells
but today focuses on
a motionless crab
    recently deceased

This solitary creature
    somehow captures my attention,
inspiring an overactive imagination
    to study a lifeless crab body
miles from the nearest dinner plate

Sitting down
    beside my newfound companion
questions cascade
from my inquisitive mind to his:
    How he felt about his life,
    Where he had traveled,
    What kind of funeral
        he always dreamed of

Clearly crabs are not prepared
to share such personal information
    with total strangers,
compelling me to seek an alternate approach,
so I psychically dive headfirst
into his diminutive shell,
then peep through lifeless claws
    to see the world through the eyes of a crab,
who wonders what all the fuss is about

Curiosity will never kill a crab,
nor will it solve his eternal problems
simple as they may be.
Temporarily inhabiting one prehistoric crab mind
I learn his greatest fear
    is being reincarnated as human
—*nature's greatest curse upon the creature kingdom*—
a surprising insight of cross-species understanding

I thank my lifeless companion
for allowing this brief cerebral trespass,
carefully extracting myself
before the rising tide washes him away

Wading ankle deep in his tidal tomb
I realize
humans are the greatest mystery of creation
confounding all other creatures
    large and small
who cannot fathom
    the meaning in life we endlessly crave
or arrogantly claim to have found

In a floating eulogy for this coffinless crab
his undersea kin collectively wonder
    "Why can't these foolish people realize
            the meaning IS life
    without need for further question or scrutiny?"
—nature's original unspoken doctrine of destiny

BACKSTORY
Eulogy For A Crab

When we show our respect for other living things,
they respond with respect for us.
—Arapaho proverb

Eulogy For A Crab was written the day after my cousin's wedding on Cape Cod. The weather was absolutely gorgeous, so I decided to hop on the Chatham Bars ferry and cross the bay to a pristine island bordering the Atlantic Ocean.

After hiking across numerous sand dunes, I arrived at ocean's edge on a deserted stretch of white sand beach. Unrolling a large hotel towel, I flopped down and stared at the crystal clear sea as it crashed against the sand. Every so often, a passing seal popped its head out of the water as if to say hello. For anyone unfamiliar with the patterns of seals in water, they are reminiscent of household pets bobbing along in leisurely dog paddle. Their facial structure and whiskers cause them to resemble friendly oversized puppies.

Every time a seal submerged, I would anxiously wait for it to resurface. If it didn't, I feared the seal had been eaten by a shark. This concern was fueled by a story in the local newspaper reporting our government has managed to tag many of the great white sharks cruising our coastal waters. Hovering in helicopters, special sharpshooters fire electronic monitors into the great whites so they can be tracked. The buzz around Cape Cod was that a number of sharks had been tracked in close proximity to local beaches. All tourists were sternly warned not to swim anywhere near seals, since seals are a favorite food source for sharks.

As I imagined the potential undersea drama of a great white shark eating one of the cuddly seals, I heard voices rise from beneath the waves. What washed into my mind was a modified Golden Rule quite different than the phrase in the Bible, which advises *"Love thy Neighbor."*
The Golden Rule of the Sea pouring into my ear was *"Eat Your Neighbor."*

All this pondering about undersea activity got me in the mood to communicate with a sea creature. However, no living creatures made themselves available as I squatted on my towel. Later that afternoon, while walking back to the boat dock, I encountered a dead crab sprawled in the sand at water's edge. This particular crab captured my imagination.

Surprisingly, words began pouring into my mind as if we were having a conversation. This interaction lasted until the tide floated the lifeless creature back to sea. As it drifted away, I pulled out my pen and attempted to immortalize the poor little crustacean.

BRAIN RIDE

It is important you know
—When strolling in city parks
I feed quarters to squirrels
just to watch them purchase bags of nuts,
then mock the lost simplicity of it all

I wrote a book once, but it was too long
    so I wrote a poem
profound as toothpaste
    using the same idea.
Meanwhile, dishes piled up in my sink,
confused by life's wreckage
    staring me in the face

Some of the most expensive real estate today
    is built on garbage.
Like this poem, it's not the odor
    people are disturbed by, but the message
so indecipherable
    even its creator needs a Rosetta Stone to unravel

What is the reason for all this verbiage?
Do poets merely take self-indulgent brain rides
then jump out of bed into a cold shower?
        NO!
It takes years of torment
    to write sloppy words on wrinkled brown grocery bags
snatched from the filthy gutter

I could talk of spectacular rainbows and leafy tree limbs
alive with the songs of a thousand feathered adornments
surrounded by glorious flowers of intoxicating colors and fragrances,
but I choose to drag you through the cobwebs of my private dungeon
    open the door, and then unceremoniously kick you out

Get out now, before it's too late
    and this confounding experience
leaves you irreversibly changed forever.
    You chuckle in conceited ignorance,
unaware the atmosphere around you has silently shifted,
    rendering you vulnerable to unknown forces

You risk the frightful fate
    of being crazed with the vision of ultimate sanity.
I know that feeling, and it hurts to understand
what everyone used to know
    life is supposed to feel like

BACKSTORY
Brain Ride

If you understand everything, you must be misinformed
—Japanese proverb

The more deeply sorrow carves into your being, the more joy you can contain.
—Kahlil Gibran

It may seem hard to believe, but I was in a very good mood when I wrote Brain Ride. I had no idea where it was headed as I began, so the swerving twists and turns it took were a surprise even to me. Allowing my pen to take charge enabled a conflicting series of images to emerge. Composing Brain Ride felt like digging up a diverse montage of artifacts from Egyptian desert sands. It also made me feel I owed readers an explanation—a proverbial Rosetta Stone to decipher what I was really thinking.

This poem seeks to provide a cerebrally stimulating adventure by blending a number of seemingly unrelated topics in a manner that evokes playful poetic spirit. Perhaps this poem should have been named *"Rollercoaster,"* because while writing, it felt like an amusement park ride in my mind. Fortunately, recent neuroscience research has revealed that chaotic mental workouts can cultivate beneficial brain plasticity.

Brain Ride forced me to contemplate my own dark side, and what a private dungeon might look like. It also made me ponder how abruptly anyone can become vulnerable to unexpected events turning their personal world upside down.

The concept of offering money to squirrels was added to exemplify the artificiality of modern urban life. It is difficult to visualize city squirrels buying bags of nuts and then meticulously burying them in specific locations as if establishing bank accounts. My main interest in depicting this bizarre transaction was to consider how squirrels might be changed by the unnatural act of purchasing their food. In absurd contemplation I pondered:

Would those squirrels figure out some miniature financial system…and would this realization inevitably cause some profound Darwinian effect on their whole species?
The extrapolation of imaginary squirrel banking activity leads to a broader curiosity regarding mankind's far-reaching effect on all other species of the world and how modern cultures mindlessly detour the flow of nature's path. As we persist in our attempt to domesticate nature, we must also realize nature is simultaneously attempting to domesticate us.

That is the real brain ride!

BULLSIGHT

Some people
need to be gored by the bull
to know what it feels like

For them
life is a bloody mess

Those
who understand pain
use mistakes of others
as helpful roadmaps
instead of waving red capes
at the horns of fate

BACKSTORY
Bullsight

A person with foresight doesn't have to experience the entire series of events to know what is likely coming.
—Norman Doidge, M.D.

Common sense is not so common.
—French proverb

Some of us learn from other people's mistakes, and the rest of us have to be other people.
—Zig Ziglar

Bullsight is dedicated to anyone who has unwittingly marched into an avoidable problem at some point in life. While each situation has its own unique elements, the common thread is an overabundance of blind optimism or foolish stubbornness. Marching through the red flags of life is a risky proposition. Only in rare instances is the outcome triumphant. Inevitably, ignoring the blaring warning signs of life leads to a painful goring by the proverbial bull.

I have learned to heed life's warning flags and thereby minimize the goring. More importantly, experience has taught me there are lessons to be learned from all mistakes. Learning the wisdom of such lessons can be a blessing in disguise. For those who insist on being gored repeatedly, life will most likely be a painful ordeal.

TOO MUCH

Caring too much is self-destructive idealism,
    a dreamer's paradise
enabling temporary escape
from throbbing inner pain

Those who care too much
    about every distant creature or thing
secretly loathe themselves,
unwittingly avoiding that nasty truth
    by creating misguided swirls of excessive emotion

Doing too much is the hyperactive brother
    of caring too much,
two siblings who regale each other daily
    over a sip of chardonnay,
toasting a slew of hollow triumphs
while avoiding their true nemesis
        feeling too much,
since without true feelings
    life is false teeth
sitting in a slimy bedside glass

BACKSTORY
Too Much

*Only those who will risk going too far
can possibly find out how far one can go.*
—T.S. Elliot

Too Much at first appears to be a poem about excess and extremes, but it is really about the importance of self-awareness. While the term *"too much"* usually refers to possessions, in this poem it refers to extreme emotions and how a lack of inner knowledge can result in serious blunders. Too Much repeatedly uses the phrase *"caring too much,"* because I have heard so many people use it without connection to true emotion. The use of *"doing too much"* is a cryptic glance at those who overwork themselves to avoid their true feelings. On the positive side, any time we can untangle our emotions and act based on true feelings, we are moving in a positive direction.

Too Much is a gentle reminder to anyone who feels overpowering emotions rising up. It is essential to understand oneself before allowing strong emotions to influence behavior. I imagined two people sitting at an outdoor café where an innocuous conversation veers out of control, resulting in a blindly emotional argument. As both combatants become overheated, it is increasingly clear neither of them know the true reason behind their argument. They are yelling at each other about a damaged watch, but the underlying basis for the anger is one of them stole the other's lover.

Unfortunately, misdirected anger and passive-aggressive behaviors are quite common in contemporary society. Experience has taught me to take time to clarify where emotions are coming from before letting them out of the bottle. Knowing where feelings come from is the best way to direct them appropriately. It is essential we do not mislead ourselves as we navigate the river of life since misguided emotions have the power to lead into dangerous territory.

NO MORE WORRY

Worry is a selfish masquerade
nobody's friend
        arising from
feelings of powerlessness and fear

Worry is lack of trust
which explains
    why people are uncomfortable
when others worry about them
—they feel distrusted by the worrier

Worry is actually about the worrier's
    secret attempt to control.
Worry never prevents disaster
since worry is a leading cause of accidents
        whenever the object of worry
    suffers paralytic distractions of self-doubt

Worry is misdirected frustration and grief
    finding their way to the surface
        disguised as caring,
at best a waste of energy,
        mostly
    worry is volatile delusion
toxically derived from secret suffering,
    a misguided insidious weapon of devastation

BACKSTORY
No More Worry

Worry, not work, kills a man.
—Maltese proverb

Worry is a misuse of imagination.
—Steve Chandler

The encyclopedia of worry is massive. I gave my copy away long ago. Worry is an invention in the mind of someone who should be thinking about something else. I hated it when my mother told me she was going to worry about me. What possible good could come out of it?

The worrier is rarely in a position to be of any assistance to the person being worried about. All the worrier can achieve is to inflict doubt upon the person who is trying to get somewhere or accomplish something. Worry is an unfortunate part of human nature better replaced by positive assistance.

Worry dampens an adventurous spirit.

Worry freezes the creative process, bringing it to a standstill.

Worry suctions the enjoyment out of someone else's life.

Knowing someone is worrying about me always makes me nervous and much more likely to make mistakes. In my adult life, I have seen the threat of worry used as a weapon, becoming a sinister method of controlling someone in an effort to stop that person from doing something the worrier doesn't want them to do. In such an instances, the worrier has little regard for the well-being of the person being worried about. Fruitless energy spent in worry is both irrational and unhealthy. All involved parties suffer as a result. Rather than suggest creative alternatives, every worrier assumes the role of self-inflicted victim. Worriers need to find some way to work off the pent up frustration they feel. Perhaps a trip to the gym or a shopping spree will suffice.

So remember, if someone's constant worry is driving you crazy, the worrier is the person who should see a therapist.

REGRETS

Regrets pour out of tattered suitcases
one old shoe at a time
until the floor is cluttered beyond recognition

Regrets, like decaying fish
are unwanted overnight guests
who stay six more months

Regrets cannot be given to charity.
They are permanent fixtures
etched in internal visions of the past
as uncensored closed circuit broadcasts
    repeating at will

Parents pass on regrets
to their children
introduced by the phrase
    "I never should have"
while those without children
bestow each regret on their unfortunate pets
    or any available ear

Regrets as a part of daily life
tell endless stories
unable to find beginnings
exclusively reserved for fearful cowards
vulnerable to inaction

Regrets are invisible death
disguised as conversation,
a waste of time
better spent
cleaning up a cluttered closet

BACKSTORY
Regrets

Regret is one of the worst human emotions.
—Bob Costas (NBC/2012 Olympics)

Having taken such a strong stand on the subject of regrets, I feel obligated to explain my position. It goes back a number of years when I heard someone utter:
"My biggest regrets are the things I never tried."
This immediately caused me to reflect on my life and recall the times I didn't try something because it seemed too risky. The list included a few special women I had been too shy to approach, and some very promising adventures I had declined to attempt. I was much more at peace with the memories of girls who had rejected me than I was with the ones I had been afraid to approach. For days the phrase about regrets reverberated within me like a huge gong struck by a flying bowling ball. I kept hearing *"the things I never tried"* over and over in my mind. From that day on, I resolved to always *"Go for it"* when an opportunity presented itself. This was one of the best decisions I have ever made.

While this landmark decision subsequently spared me innumerable regrets in my own life, I have since listened to barrelfuls of regrets pouring out of the mouths of most everyone I encounter. So many of the regrets people express arise from lingering insecurities that have stopped them in their tracks. Unfortunately, human nature frequently blinds people to the potential rewards of trying new experiences, leaving those individuals regretting much. This conjured up the image of a cluttered closet. Open the closet door, and everything spills out to create a cluttered floor. The good thing about a cluttered floor is it forces a person to clean it up. A cluttered mind is much more difficult to clear. Clutter up a mind with too many regrets, and it cannot function properly. Even worse, the process of regretting then interferes with solving the real problem.

Writing backstories for Regrets and No More Worry highlighted my extreme distaste for these two mental states. After considerable analysis, it appears regrets and worry have a symbiotic relationship, as worry often restricts activity, which leaves an individual prone to developing regrets. Conversely, a person with many regrets is most likely a worrier.

Now you know why I dislike regrets. I definitely would have regretted it if I did not include this poem in my book.

DANCING WITH BOGART

Have you ever met someone
    who was so far away emotionally
        you had to be there with them
just once, in a flash
    to never be the same?

Her lonely shadow emerges
    from the past
craving a part in this man's tragedy,
desperately attracted
    by his magnet of indifference

Cigarette butts and whiskey
    surround this distant fog of a man
one tobacco-filled kiss after another
    bathing in the masochistic splendor
of an empty sweetheart
dancing the ultimate fox trot
    step after step
with someone
    who will never fully open his heart
on or off the silver screen

BACKSTORY
Dancing With Bogart

A number of years ago, I attended a three-day seminar hosted by the legendary Robert McKee, who is internationally acclaimed for his brilliant lectures and books on the art of screenwriting. On the seminar's final day, Mr. McKee used the movie Casablanca as his example of the perfect movie screenplay. More than two hundred of us studied every word spoken in Casablanca for more than six hours, analyzing each character in great detail.

Humphrey Bogart's Rick Blaine made a deep impression on me. Rick operated in a fog, as an empty shadow of himself. His character possesed a liquid quality that could not be pinpointed. This liquid aspect of his personality seemed capable of evaporating into thin air at any time. He was friends with everyone, yet nobody actually knew him at all.

Rick was a colorful fellow who possessed impeccable integrity, yet in many ways he didn't have any personality. In a bizarre paradox, Rick was more alive than everyone around him, yet it seemed something in Rick had died long ago. He kept deflecting his own desires for his principles to the point where he knowingly put his own life in grave jeopardy. At the same time, Rick was absolutely inscrutable, arranging to save Victor Laszlo, who was taking away the love of Rick's life forever.

In facilitating the escape of Ilsa Lund—Rick's great love from the past—Rick also rescued her husband by providing safe passage out of Casablanca. It seemed as though Rick banished his only chance at lasting love because he couldn't stand the pain of having to love someone again. Rick was happier remembering one great week in Paris than trying to find a way to repeat it. Ilsa was still in love with Rick and was torn to shreds by all this, yet Rick remained cool as ice, choosing the moral high road in preserving Ilsa's marriage to a man she no longer seemed to love. This unspoken conflict created the gripping good-bye scene between Rick and Ilsa on the airport tarmac where Rick uttered the classic movie line, *"We'll always have Paris."*

Marveling at a person who could be so detached from his own predicament, I was moved to write this poem, which somehow reminds me of an emotionally charged slow fox trot. I also wondered what kind of man Bogart must have been to inhabit Rick's persona, and what type of woman would be drawn to such a man.

LOVESWAMP

As if a lost submarine,
having spent years
in aimless undersea adventure,
ballast tanks suddenly blow
precipitating an unexpectedly rapid ascent
to surface at the edge
of a vast murky swamp

Breaking through water's crust
with a startling splash,
weeds stream across my face,
dangle from my torso,
as I test solid ground
for the first time in years

Where am I?
No…Where have I been?
And why?
How could I have accepted
so many misguided years of submergence
without protest,
wallowing in muck
that always grows deeper
when what one calls love
is truly a swamp

BACKSTORY
Loveswamp

Loveswamp was written in a reflective moment while examining the way I had conducted my love life for decades. Relationships always started out splendidly but inevitably managed to end up in the proverbial swamp. It took many years of wallowing in the muck to realize there was a part of me that had been secretly unwilling to become fully vulnerable. Unwittingly, I was clinging to an invisible safety net at all times. Perhaps I sensed the net was necessary because I hadn't yet found the right person. Fortunately, by the time I wrote Loveswamp, I was already out of the weeds.

Loveswamp seeks to assist those who suffer with failing relationships. It officially launched my new perspective on love, which can be summed up by this quote:

"Those who seek emotional safety in love are guaranteed to find disappointment."

Intimate relationships require us to look within ourselves before concluding our partner is at fault. If you truly love your partner, make sure you are not fooling yourself about your commitment and full involvement.

A full surrender is necessary.

That is the only way to get out of the swamp forever.

SELF PORTRAIT

I am already ten days late by the time I am born with a doctor's slap.
Being late for birth is not by mistake…I wanted to stay in there as long as possible, making sure not to miss anything, since I know there's no going back later.
It is my first game plan, and I haven't yet been born.
I am two years old. It's the first bad day of my life because Mother goes away looking very upset. She won't tell me where she is going, and then she doesn't come home for dinner. She doesn't come home for dinner for more than two months. Nobody tells me what's wrong. If she is fine like they say, then Mommy must want to leave me, so I feel abandoned…and I am born.
This paranoia will last for years.
Mother returns from the hospital and life is almost fine, except I can't stop worrying she might go away again. I watch Mommy like a hawk. At the age of six, she takes me to a city swimming pool in a neighborhood park. I bring my goggles to swim. The sign says

"NO GOGGLES ALLOWED."

I look at the pool and see other children wearing goggles. Being polite, I ask the lifeguard if I can wear goggles when I swim.
He says, *"No!"*
So I ask him why the kids in the pool are allowed to wear goggles.
He says, *"Because they didn't ask."*
Once again, I am born.
No more self-defeating questions.
Our family goes to the beach. I always swim with a flotation tube. For some reason, on this day I forget to wear my tube. My mother notices this detail and is thrilled to see me swim like a grownup. She shouts at me how wonderful it is I am swimming without a tube. That piece of information puts me in a panic and I immediately begin to drown.
As a large man rescues me to shore, I am born.
I have learned I can do what I cannot believe I can do.
Self-doubt can drown a life.
When I am seventeen, Grandma is killed by a gypsy cab running a red light in the Bronx. She is so mangled, her coffin must be kept closed. I am moved to write a eulogy.
When I read it at her funeral, everyone's eyes fill with tears, and I am born.
A lifetime of speech writing begins at Grandma's funeral.
I am twenty-two years old and away at college. The telephone rings at 3am.
My aunt's shaky voice introduces the unspeakable nightmare: *My father is dead.*
His heart suddenly failed him prematurely at age fifty-eight.
I am calm. I am always calm. How could anyone be so incredibly calm?
What am I made of?
The next morning I fly home to help my mother pick up the pieces. A stranger opens my mother's door and I enter an oil painting draped in black. My mother is frozen with grief, so I write another eulogy, and once again I am born.
I instantly become my father for my mother, and am there for her as she has

been there for me forever. Words never need be spoken. This relationship endures longer than my parents knew each other, as my mother lives another thirty-six years.

My father's early death gives birth to a lifelong dread of my own premature demise.

A few years later I am poisoned by a doctor's prescription, and I am born. Questioning the medical profession will save my life one day.

I fall in love, but she eventually drifts away while I sit helpless as a snail in pursuit of a racecar. Once again, I am born.

I soon learn to entice racecars to drive in my direction so I don't have to chase after them. A flood of lovers parades my way, but unfortunately I am still in love with the shadow of my first racecar. Her shadow hangs over me for two more decades while I blindly go through the motions of love. My body is alert while my spirit absorbs the diverse mosaic of life.

I am ready for it all. I am always ready.

How could anyone always be so incredibly ready all the time?

I say yes to every offer life presents me, and am continually being born.

Learning the world opens to those who embrace it without fear, I inwardly thank my parents for nurturing me sufficiently to live a fearless life.

My game plan thrives by changing daily to adapt in every situation.

This fearless life glides on a magic carpet for years, until one rainy afternoon an aging car runs a red light and crashes into mine. I am forty-four.

The ninety-two-year-old man driving the other car says he was confused by the weather. They put him in an ambulance as I limp around my crumbled automobile.

Physical pain doesn't begin immediately, but then it never goes away.

Once again I am born, as pain becomes my teacher.

This new pain leads me in never-imagined directions that eventually change every cell of my body. The medical profession offers me pain-killing medications, which I refuse as I embrace alternative medicine.

I want to feel everything. I want to stay pure.

I learn a bit of all I never knew, and I am born.

This birth feels different. This time, I embrace the compassionate concept of gratitude as my mind heals my body and rejuvenates my soul.

I am betrayed by a business associate who has masqueraded as my best friend for many years. Instead of becoming bitter, I ask how I can help him with his unhappiness. Within two years, he develops cancer and dies.

Despite his betrayal, I compose a glowing eulogy for him.

Everyone deserves a graceful exit.

The impact of these painful experiences touches my heart. I realize how little has touched my heart for a long time. I stop asking the universe for a woman who loves me and start asking for a woman I can truly love.

Looking back, it tears me apart that my mind, body and spirit had all been working overtime to make up for the tragic fact my heart was frozen by a middle-of-the-night phone call when I was twenty-two years old and still chasing the shadow of my first unreachable love. With all subsequent thinking, I can't believe I had not found a way to use my heart to its fullest. My words failed to express the rich feelings of love and caring I felt for the world, so one peaceful evening, I cuddled up with my thoughts while chewing a golden-yellow apricot. While it melted in my mouth, the apricot sternly whispered,

"You have found God…just stop denying it, and give in to a universe that wants to embrace you as much as you unwittingly desire to embrace it."

I opened my mouth long enough to promise the apricot from that moment on my heart would be fully engaged and ready to fill my life with the love it secretly craved ever since that bleak December day they put my father into his coffin.

I am finally born to make this prediction: *"The scale of hearts has tipped forever."* Years later I pick up the story of my prehistoric life and read it. Seeing this prediction feels like viewing the writings of Nostradamus as I realize the scale of my heart has tipped exactly as forecasted.

The miracle of it all is when my heart opened, a wonderful woman rushed in to give it a hug. She promised never to leave, just to make sure I've learned my lesson. Together we found a house with a swimming pool, so now I can wear my goggles. I no longer worry about my destination as I am here, and that is where I wish to stay.

I have truly been born, and it all began the day I opened my heart.

TOMORROW'S PLAN

She sat alone,
a stunning blond portrait
   hair blowing longer than the breeze

It was just another day at the beach
till he passed her majestic smile
   and shyly asked for the time

She didn't know, but was kind enough to say so
as he trudged past the goddess of his dreams
   without making further attempt

Refreshed by this brief encounter,
his night was filled with amorous dreams of her
replaying her sweet response
   now topped with the cherry of his own romantic fantasy

His scheme to win her heart now complete
next morning he marched confidently back
to her location on the beach,
   now occupied by a hungry seagull in search of breakfast

Unfortunately, only a trail of footprints
adorned her vacated sandy spot,
lonely remnants of the painful lesson
   that tomorrow's plan is best enacted today

TOMORROW NEVER COMES

When today
waits for tomorrow
it disappears in future's shadow

Reach back to grab a slice of yesterday
—you stub your toe on tomorrow—
a lesson taught by dead friends and relatives
whose memories are best viewed
as stepping stones to the future,
not silhouettes parked in the rearview mirror of life

Today is not
the average of yesterday and tomorrow,
it is a vibrant slice of forever,
the only true reality

BACKSTORY
Tomorrow's Plan & Tomorrow Never Comes

Today is the tomorrow we worried about yesterday.
—Grant Schreiber

Act boldly and unseen forces will come to your aid.
—Dorothea Brande

These two poems arose from contemplating the concept of living in the present moment. At first glance, both poems seem to be rehashing the same theme, but closer inspection reveals some differences. The following short paragraph inspired this duo of Tomorrow poems:

Today, fully lived
Leads me boldly to my future
Today, not fully lived
Slides me unwittingly
Back to my past

Fundamentally, Tomorrow's Plan illustrates a specific incident that leads to a realization about the value dealing with life in real time. Tomorrow Never Comes is the same person talking to himself after suffering through the experience depicted in Tomorrow's Plan.

One of my favorite words in the English language is the word *'now'*. I take *now* very seriously. Tackling challenges and responsibilities with a *"do it now"* attitude keeps life from piling up or drifting away. It clears the mind as well as the *"to do"* list. In essence, the thrust of these two poems is:

Today is *"now"*, yesterday is *"then"* and tomorrow is *"whenever"*.

In other words, yesterday is history and tomorrow is the realm of possibilities. As the poem states, today is the only reality.

THE WIDOW

There it was,
just like the movies
she stands shrouded in black
legs glued to the floor
trembling
with no appetite
except to cry
   or look at old snapshots
repeating her desperate prayer
   "may yesterday return again"

Life's equation once solved
now doesn't add up to
half a loaf of stale bread
with years more
left to rot
   as her own jail keeper
still sleeping on her side
   of an empty double bed
craving the reassuring snores
   of her deceased companion
whose grave she frequently visits
hoping to soon join him in permanent residence

BACKSTORY
The Widow

Grief can take care of itself, but to get the full value of a joy
you must have somebody to divide it with.
—Mark Twain

I dedicate The Widow to all those who have lost loved ones. The original picture in my mind was the condition of my own mother the day after my father suddenly passed away, but I have since witnessed numerous friends, relatives, and acquaintances shortly after the sudden death of a soul mate. Recently, I walked into my local bank and noticed the most cheerful teller in a rare state of disarray. This usually effervescent woman could barely mumble a hello as I stepped up to her counter. I looked around to see if something else might be causing her inexplicably muted demeanor. As she mechanically took my deposit in a manner devoid of her usual jovial vitality, I searched her humorless face for a clue. When she handed me my deposit receipt, she managed to whisper that her husband had suddenly died the week before and this was her first day back at work. Clearly, she was still in the grips of a major trauma no person can fully prepare for.

The Widow attempts to burrow inside the mind of a person still suffering from such a loss. It does not venture beyond the initial condition of inconsolable grief to demonstrate the resilience most people exhibit as time passes. In the unfortunate case of the elderly widow described in this poem, the trauma became permanent, and her sole source of comfort was the thought of reuniting with her beloved deceased husband.

If this widow was a poet, she may have written the following while sitting in her favorite chair:

For decades
we wrote the poem of life together.
You were every other line
and I was the rest
until your pen ran out of ink
leaving me like coffee without the cup

I still boil with the idea of us
but now my pot is full of tears
knowing no monologue of love
can ever bring you back

GRANDFATHER'S CLOCK

Echoes die in this old house as if corpses in a morgue.
    Silent roars of deceased relatives
interrupted only by the incessant tick of Grandfather's clock,
that monumental timepiece
outliving generations of mothers, fathers, children, and grandchildren
    to conquer this once-noble home with humble persistence

Some heirlooms gather dust and fungus
while others develop awesome strength
derived from years of vigilant service.
Through creaky floorboards, Grandfather's clock
    has grown the roots of an elm.
Long after my rocking chair squeals its last sleepy song,
an earthquake may someday demolish its moldy surroundings
    but Grandfather's clock will never budge an inch

As lone guardian of this tomb
I strain to remember
when these walls reverberated with youthful vigor,
    but my days are slowly fading.
Last week the phone rang once
  —It was my grandson—
    Strangely enough, nothing seems trivial to that boy.
We talk forever
as my eighty years of life flow between us like a river
he listens to my yarns as if touched by a god,
    not realizing he is my God as well

I finally put down the phone
then reminisce with Grandfather's clock
    how in youth
love and lust overwhelmed all else
replaced in middle age by cravings for money and power
    followed by futile attempts to achieve immortal security

Now, as an aging warrior
I cherish memories of friends long since buried
while savoring each glorious moment
    one precious tick at a time

BACKSTORY
Grandfather's Clock

Grandfather's Clock is not about the clock. It's about the person listening to the clock. After writing The Widow, I slipped into the mental state of imagining myself as an elderly man who senses the curtain coming down on his life. To compound the image, I placed myself in an ancient family home filled with memorabilia from past generations. I then imagined everyone had already forgotten about me except one grandson, who was too young to understand my condition. In conjuring up all these images, I heard the ticking of a clock. Closing my eyes, I began to survey the implications of such a dire situation.

This poem is about being stuck. I have a vehement disdain for items of nostalgia that slowly entomb those who collect them. It is a sinister trap arising from misguided materialism that strangles the life out of each victim one dustball at a time. Envisioning myself declining in an old creaky house made me very sad.

Most of all, it made me feel sad for all the people who actually live such an isolated existence. It also honed my determination never to let this happen to me. Just thinking about this poem motivates me to rush into the garage and throw something out.

FINAL CHILD ORPHANS CLUB

Upon losing their final parent
people instantly become orphans
with no remedy
     no cure
     no way back
except in minds that rehash memories
of previously unshattered worlds

This tragic truth garners no sympathy
from those whose parents continue to live
until fate throws each newly traumatized descendant
into steaming pots of orphan stew

A child is never whole again
after losing a parent.
There is always a hole,
an ache of great loss tugging at one's soul,
   the hole
     the ache
expands geometrically with loss of a final parent
no matter what one's age

All dead parents were children once,
children who survived
profound pain of losing their parents
   only to learn
dead parents never really die,
  —They secretly inhabit all offspring—
Eternally thrashing within their minds

The passage of endless time barely blinks
   as each child grows to become a parent
      before owning dead parents of their own,
each set of dead relations
   pulsing through veins of the next generation
      until one orphan fails to procreate,
breaking the chain,
   ending the long line of suffering
by dying without offspring
     slowly sliding into the dark void
with no one around to shed a tear

Each final child leaves sadly without encore
   never to experience
the climactic glory of becoming a dead parent
  -a universal birthright of an optimistic species

BACKSTORY
Final Child Orphans Club

Final Child Orphans Club was triggered by the death of my mother thirty-six years after the death of my father. Her death brought on the odd feeling of being an orphan even though I was a middle-aged adult. In speaking to a number of others, I learned I was not alone. Almost every person who had lost both parents shared this uncomfortable feeling.

Feeling like an orphan was simultaneously compounded by the knowledge my wife and I would never have children of our own. It was as though my mind was looking up and looking down at the same time but seeing only a vacuum. Two years later, my wife's father died. At the age of ninety-seven, he had outlived his wife of sixty years by a decade. Suddenly, my wife was an orphan as well. One evening, we began discussing this phenomenon—how people can feel orphaned at any age, how the loss of all parents is a permanent change altering one's position in their intimate world, and how the shift caused by this inevitable change rarely dawns on anyone until it occurs.

In the midst of discussing the issue of parental loss with my wife, I happened to mention I was the final child of my lineage. The words *"final child"* reverberated in my head during a mostly sleepless night that led me to slide out of bed and stagger down to my office. As I turned on the desk lamp to write down a few words, my pen refused to stop, so I flopped into a chair and the surging feelings flowed through my hand.

Final Child Orphans Club is probably the saddest poem I have ever written, mainly because I am a member. This poem portrays the two biggest challenges in life I have never been able to conquer: keeping my parents alive and having children of my own.

I always assumed I would become a father at some point in time. Not having children haunts me at times, since it deprives me of an ability to leave the abundance of my existence to a direct descendant. It makes me wonder how silent it might be when the final curtain comes down on my life. At the same time, this empty feeling fuels me to attempt to do as much good as possible while I'm still alive.

A LEAF'S LIFE

As springtime's clock
   begins to tick
nature once again
   moves front and center
displaying her vast arsenal of beauty,
a verdant galaxy
brightening the palette of existence
   with spring's vibrant song of rebirth

Each bud on bush or tree
represents a life
   a hope
   a wish
   a dream,
each leaf contains an untold story
finding purpose
   by shading us from sweltering summer sun
then taking autumn's earthward drift
to transform itself into fertile soil
   ready to nourish all the world's creatures

Is it possible leaves contemplate each phase of their brief life cycle?
Are they aware of the indispensable services they so selflessly render?
Do they possess a language of their own?
Does the crunch underfoot of a resting leaf signify a cry of pain?
Does the whistle of a breeze denote an exclamation of joy?

Perhaps autumn's brilliant colors
are Mother Nature's secret coded messages
   informing us
a leaf's life is precious
   as any other in the entire universe

BACKSTORY
A Leaf's Life

Nature, to be commanded, must be obeyed.
—Sir Francis Bacon

Francis Bacon wrote these words more than four hundred years ago. Today they are more poignant than ever. The arrogant belief we can somehow dictate revised laws of nature to our world is clearly self-destructive. As my love of nature grows, I am constantly struck by this truth and the need to work with nature to reach a mutually beneficial balance. In A Leaf's Life, I chose to reverently study the plant kingdom by following the life of a leaf.

It is very easy to overlook the life of an individual leaf. Very rarely are leaves pictured as individuals. They are usually referred to as a large group, either attached to a tree or laying helplessly on the ground. Focusing on each leaf as an entity experiencing a life of its own created a radically different vision. An anthropomorphic renaissance took place in my mind in reference to leaves. As humans, we can easily fall into the limited view of assuming only humans have feelings, thoughts, or a purpose. When we entertain the concept of all living things having these attributes, a new universe of possibilities opens up. Nature blossoms into a splendorous wonderland of profound creatures and environments in which every complex interaction has its precious place as part of a unified vibrant mosaic.

SUMMER IN AUTUMN

Nature's kaleidoscope
    carries soft breezes
through each tree limb across Mother Earth
as a royal procession of glorious October sun
graces every creature
    with summer's last embrace

A treasure in every breath
abounding from nature's bosom,
the rapture of a precious day
    to be savored
as reward we deserve for surviving all the others

This special day
becomes a day to
    stop
    enjoy
    inhale
celebrate with gratitude and hope
    enchanting sweetness
while each deep breath fills with sacred beauty,
    aromatic doses of healing medicine
for body and soul
    absorbing
    soaking
    rejoicing
each miraculous moment

Evoking an affirmation for all:
    May you recognize nature's philanthropy
    and when it arrives,
    may you have enough wisdom to seize
    each rare opportunity to bathe in divine beauty

Nature's boundless immense wealth
    given freely,
the astonishing restorative power
    of leisure time well spent

BACKSTORY
Summer In Autumn

If you are losing your leisure, look out!
You may be losing your soul.
—Logan Pearsall Smith

Summer in Autumn started out to simply be a celebration of the wonders of nature, but ended up pointing to something else. As I frolicked through a glorious autumn day, it became apparent many people never take the time to do so. I observed hordes of people hustling and bustling but never looking up to absorb the natural beauty of the panorama I was so enamored with. This shifted my focus from nature to the value of leisure time. While nature is always present and constantly invites us to indulge ourselves, it is our responsibility to partake of the abundance being offered, especially when Mother Nature brews up one of her exceptionally wondrous days.

I redesigned the ending of this poem to nudge those who have allowed life's pressures to supersede the call of the wild. Leisure time is not merely a luxury; it is an essential component of a sustainable healthy life. Hopefully, Summer in Autumn's cheerful call to action will not be ignored.

GREEN THUMBS

I owned a cactus once
but gave it too much water.
It died,
so I bought some succulent ferns,
carefully rationing their water supply
    until they perished from severe thirst

After that loss
I couldn't stand myself
    or the thought of plants.
Life was an ongoing funeral
    until one day
a thirsty woman spoke of her deceased foliage,
embracing me with a nurturing warmth
    that turned all our thumbs green

Now we live in a thriving garden
having learned
with balance
    wilted plants can come back to life

BACKSTORY
Green Thumbs

Your partner is a flower.
If you take care of her well, she will grow beautifully.
If you take care of her poorly, she will wither.
To help a flower grow well, we must understand her nature.
How much water does she need? How much sunshine?
—Thich Nhat Hanh

Just so you know, I really did ruin my favorite cactus plant by giving it too much water, and really did accidentally kill some treasured plants by not giving them enough to drink. Fortunately, I learned how to take care of my plants soon after those two upsetting experiences. But the vital lesson of this poem is not about plants.

It is about people.
It is about love.
It is about relationships.
It is about the encouraging truth it is never too late in life to find happiness.

Green Thumbs views the quest to find fulfilling love as a dynamic lifelong opportunity. Desire for this state of being often requires substantial changes in behavior and mental outlook. My various relationships with plants emerged as a prime metaphor to illuminate this very important truth. The key challenge was learning how to apply a newly acquired green thumb with plants to the rest of my life. Indulging the plant metaphor clarified two vastly different phases present in all love relationships: *Finding love vs. Growing love.*
Finding love can be equated to purchasing a beautiful plant.
The *growing love* phase begins the moment you bring your new plant home, as a relationship has begun. A balance needs to be established. If you nurture your plant properly, it will respond by beautifying your home. Mature love between humans is more complicated, but the concept remains intact.

Green Thumbs is ultimately about attending to the needs of others, be it plants, people, pets, or any other meaningful relationship. This includes paying attention to one's inner self. Balance is a byproduct of paying attention to all phases of existence, since when one's awareness is wisely spread across the spectrum of life, balance finds its way into the equation.

HERMIT SAGA

Who leaves first when two hermits meet?
   How long does a clam open to get a suntan?
     – Quickly, without fanfare –

Without warning,
It happened one afternoon
   under a schizophrenic sky
     puffed with clouds and brilliant sun
as an alienated being sat tentatively beside me
   yet kept her distance
     and just like the sky
it was difficult to say whether clouds or sun prevailed
   since each fleeting embrace
     also breathed hints of good-bye

How does one committed to indifference show interest?
   How many clams have suntans?
Shaken bottles of champagne cannot be poured slowly
   and many times all is lost
     in the unsure affections of a moment

Inspired by the whim
   there may still be someone in this world
     to give me more than I could imagine,
I let her smile echo a tantalizing challenge to discard my shell
   in the vibrant hope
     I had finally found a partner

BACKSTORY
Hermit Saga

If you close or armor the heart in order to be in the universe,
you have become a crippled instrument for the healing of the universe.
—Ram Dass

I have been one of the two hermits in this poem. I was an emotional hermit and didn't even know it. Encountering someone who was more of a hermit helped me understand my own 'hermitness'. Having a hermit mirror stare me in the face for a while proved very beneficial, as I was able to identify some of my own shortcomings by observing her. Although the relationship did not survive, the lessons of it did.

I am grateful to my hermit counterpart for teaching me much about myself by simply being herself. It cured me of being a hermit, as I saw how self-defeating such behavior can be. While a protective shell may be effective against weapons intended to do harm, the same shell unwittingly also repels the blessings of love.

The challenge is to learn when to shed one's shell to absorb all the sweetness life can offer.

SEDUCED BY A DREAM

Don't shrink from the stunning realization
I am your dream
—please let me penetrate deeper,
softly twisting inside your ecstasy

Don't analyze our inexplicable joy,
intergalactic sensations
harmonizing
   over
   under
   throughout
and ultimately upon
your sultry surface

Death sets a seductively flowered table
for bees in search of heavenly nectar,
mirroring thirsty human souls
who writhe in timeless fantasies of romantic exploration
   both at work and play,
over and over again tasting sweetness
   only to spit it out
ignorant as we are about love,
   foolishly embracing hollow logs
while full ones drift away

Passionately we join our souls
share our bodies
while swirling questions scream
   Is this it?
   The one?
   The time?
   The place?

Until love replaces doubt
we are all climbers trudging up life's cliff.
It matters not whether we limp, crawl, or hop
nor what fashion statement is made along the way,
the only judge of our journey is how it feels,
   so please
don't shrink from the stunning realization
I am your dream
because you are also mine
and nothing will ever feel like this with anyone else

BACKSTORY
Seduced By A Dream

Seduced By A Dream has a unique origin. It arose from an accumulation of phrases stored in a file titled "Spare Parts." My spare parts file consisted of a large number of original phrases I was unable to build complete poems around. Rather than throw these unused phrases away, I stored them for possible future use. In the midst of compiling *Younger & Wiser*, I opened the spare parts file to see if any might spark my imagination.

The phrase that inspired Seduced By A Dream became its opening line.

"Don't shrink from the stunning realization I am your dream."

The spare parts folder soon became a personal toolbox, with numerous other phrases blending into various poems. As Seduced By A Dream took shape, I began to realize it told the retrospective story of the evolution of my relationship with my wife. We both began our journey together as outsiders to the concept of all-encompassing love. It took a few years of struggling to finally immerse ourselves in the full beauty of deep intimacy.

All the struggling somehow textured our relationship like a fine wine benefiting from some extra aging. Once we both comprehended the miracle we were living, it began to resemble the stunning realization I had written about many years before. Clearly, when originally writing that phrase, I was not yet ready for such a profound love relationship even though I believed I was.

With my wife's approval, I include Seduced By a Dream in this book with carte blanche for anyone who wishes to introduce it to a potential lover.

For those who take advantage of this offer, be prepared for the thrill of a lifetime.

LET ME

Let me open my faucets upon you
then lend you my umbrella,
let me addict you to my touch
without upsetting your balance,
let me invade your existential privacy
    leaving you more yourself than ever

But as you observe
my sometimes awkward approach
please do not fear the happiness you give me
or search for hidden price tags
    that do not exist

Experience has taught me
love is a gift that grows only when given,
too painful when withheld
so
let me explain just this once,
the only goal
is to experience our potential,
climb the imaginary mountain
and finally
    breathe some sacred air

LOVE'S TIPPING POINT

There comes a moment
paramount in human relations
when the fullest dimensions of love
reveal themselves to a select few
who allow life's greatest miracle
its chance to grow

Transcending imagination
loving hands cannot resist
endless urges to massage
because of who is on the other end
of each fingertip,
while beyond the physical realm
deeper spheres of beauty
beckon inspiration's blind leap
through the divine portal
of love's transformative ubiquity

THE DAY US WAS BORN

The day us was born
    was like no other,
beginning innocently enough
yet concluding with worlds
    forever changed

She absorbed the story of my life
    as if she'd lived it herself
while I surgically extracted
delicate secrets of her swerving journey
    now landed at my door

Re-awakened,
we gently probed surfaces
shrouding cavernous warmth below
weightlessly soaring on destiny's carpet
    into the core of our magical selves,
two heavenly bodies suddenly transformed
    hurtling through vast galaxies
        inside each other's eyes

There was only one way to travel
    —*Into the light*—
allowing promises of ultimate joy to melt all fear,
    a vision unthinkably remote
before this blessing stopped the passage of time

Humbled, my eyes squeezed shut
to pray that truth
    not illusion
surround us with sweet love
    day and night
into eternity and beyond

BACKSTORY
The Day Us Was Born

We can only learn to love by loving.
—Doris Murdock

There is no enemy for one who keeps the radiant light of the sun in his heart.
—Rick Jarow (translation of ancient Sanskrit proverb)

The Day Us Was Born is a story of great romance. It requires very little backstory assistance, as it accurately depicts the process of entering into a love relationship. Such journeys begin tentatively at first, but as they blossom, the expansion becomes increasingly geometric. Before true love entered, I could not imagine its infinite dimensions or how it would change my perspective on every aspect of life.

Love has the power to make every minute of existence feel heavenly. All other troubles become secondary once the pure devotion of your mate is properly absorbed. Such deep, all-encompassing intimacy makes it much easier to live with grace, which has always been a primary goal.

WHEN THE FIRST TIME CAME AGAIN

When the first time came again
   I didn't see stars
     or hear bells,
just sat and cried for joy
   to know
that electrifying feeling could come again

No surprises this time
   just the thrill of witnessing
   veins stand up taller than before
to help this wilting tree
   bear fruit once again

BACKSTORY
When The First Time Came Again

Trust that the universe is working for and with you.
—Sanaya Roman

When The First Time Came Again was written in a joyful moment celebrating the realization it is never too late for true love. After numerous intimate relationships ending in disappointment, I was elated to encounter this miraculous truth later in life.

Rather than lamenting failed relationships, it is far more productive to learn from them. For anyone who is *"down in the dumps"* because past love affairs or marriages have disintegrated, please take heart that whenever you are ready, there is a good chance love will find its way back into your life. The key to this wondrous process is readiness.

Although there is no official checklist to judge such readiness, when you are ready it will be apparent to others. I call this psychic sensibility *romantic radar.* Qualities that attract romantic radar are sincerity, humbleness, openness, and compassion. As stated in the poem The Search, my unwavering motto regarding the quest for love is: *"Never give up!"*

It is reassuring to know first times can come again and be even more fulfilling the second time around..

FINE FEATHERED LOVERS

From my perch I look down
    and see you clearly.
From your perch you look up
    and say you see me clearly too

Then through ruffled feathers
I correctly deny your faulty vision
    and you deny mine
as we fruitlessly squawk to no avail
each knowing
the only time we are both correct
is when we rest our tired beaks
    on the same perch
and close our critical eyes

BACKSTORY
Fine Feathered Lovers

If you judge people, you have no time to love them.
—Mother Teresa

It is not necessary to understand things in order to argue about them.
—Beaumarchais

Love does not consist in gazing at each other,
but in looking together in the same direction.
—Antoine de Saint-Exupery

Fine Feathered Lovers is anything but subtle as it takes a firm stand on the perilous consequences of being judgmental in a love relationship. I wrote it during a difficult time in my life. While this poem focuses on how suspending judgment allows love to flow, one can easily extrapolate such an effect into a myriad of other interpersonal situations, including the workplace. Judgmental behavior is a crippler to any human endeavor, and must be differentiated from the articulation of an opinion. Once judgmental behavior pollutes a relationship, all productive conversation is terminated.

Wrestling with this type of destructive behavior once derailed a budding romance. As a post mortem to that relationship, I decided to express my strong opinion on the pitfalls of judgmental thinking. By then, I had already comprehended the antidote for such a condition is listening with an open mind.

Colorful bird images appeared in my mind, with two birds perched side-by-side in a cage. At first, the whole issue ruffled my feathers, but after years of squawking I finally took my own advice.

TO THE POINT

Throughout a laborious lifetime
of making points,
we are left to wonder
what the true point is,
straining to grasp the final point
yet finding no points
     to have any point at all

The greatest minds of many millennia
have pondered this dilemma,
concluding in a sea of disagreement
     true meaning
is a pointless destination
     well worth the effort

BACKSTORY
To The Point

Every point in the cosmos can be considered its center.
—Dorothy Maclean

To the Point is a short poem prying open a very large Pandora's Box.
After much contemplation, it arrives at more questions than answers.
The only statement likely to find widespread agreement is:
    The true meaning of life is up for interpretation at all times.
Within any debate on the meaning of life exists the possibility life's true
meaning is only realized by pursuing searches for that elusive meaning. I have
periodically wrestled with this vexing dilemma. Even the starting point is
confusing, as I am not even certain what question is best to ask.
    Should the question be: *"Does life have meaning?"*
    Or should the question be: *"What is the meaning of life?"*
This has been a great stumbling point for me, reminiscent of the chicken and the
egg. If one acknowledges life does have meaning, then the choices of what gives
life meaning become the topic for debate.
    The next question in this line of thinking is: *"Who decides what is meaningful?"*
This question complicates matters, since what is meaningful to one person
may be meaningless to another. So, how do we judge if a person has lived a
meaningful life or not? Perhaps only the person living that life can determine
the meaningfulness achieved.
    At this point, a deeper question emerges: *"What is meaningful?"*
Once again, the answer is unmanageably subjective and open for debate.
In posing these questions, I continually end up back at the original question,
    "Does life have meaning?"
Surprisingly, I cannot find any proof it does, although I desperately want to
believe there is meaning in life.
So, what is my point in hashing through all this mental wrangling?
    To the Point puts my mind at rest regarding the subject of life's meaning by
concluding if a person feels his or her life has meaning, then it does—to that
person. If someone feels another person's life has meaning, then it does—to the
person who feels it is meaningful. The same logic holds true when analyzing
events of all magnitudes; however, in the absolute sense of believing existence
has a larger meaning in some eclectic universal sense—I am skeptical.
    Although the tapestry of nature seems to be brilliantly woven together for
some incomprehensible reason, I am unable to pinpoint what it is. Therefore, the
meaning of life is a subject to be contemplated for eternity, and until we arrive at
the end of eternity, this fundamental question will continue to perplex humanity.
In a strange way, that struggle gives meaning to life!

MORNING AFFIRMATION

Thank you for this day.
I will make the most of it I possibly can

May I have the wisdom
     strength
     and fortitude
to live this day with grace

BACKSTORY
Morning Affirmation

Morning Affirmation is a phrase I say every morning before breakfast. It is part of the code I live by. Whenever I feel myself waver from this simple affirmation, I stop and take a deep breath, because it means I have drifted off course. Innumerable challenges encountered over the years have taught me profound lessons. I have learned that living with grace stabilizes all other aspects of life, and the manner in which I behave in any situation is more important than what I accomplish. It is my hope living with grace will always lead to the correct destination and best outcome.

While I offer this morning affirmation for your use, if it doesn't fit, I encourage you to create or adopt your own personal affirmation. The use of affirmations is an exceptional tool in giving life direction and form. Affirmations are powerful reminders capable of helping us forge our path to long-term goals. As I get older, I find deep pleasure in distilling down my beliefs into phrases that encapsulate the pillars of existence and assist in merging all beliefs and actions into a more cohesive overall code of conduct.

LIFE AND DEATH

All those still living are rich.
    Just ask dead billionaires
no longer able to spend their wealth
    or complain about the difficulties of life

So vexing
    is the concept of nonexistence
we unconsciously blur our vision of life,
failing to appreciate
the preciousness of each breath
    no matter what our predicament

BACKSTORY
Life And Death

Life can only be understood backward, but it must be lived forward.
—Soren Kierkegaard

Death is a subject I have yet to fully grasp.
Most of us are so busy with day-to-day life, there isn't time to decide how we feel about death. Without getting into a lengthy discussion about reincarnation, it seems the uncertainty of how death might feel actually compels us to concentrate on living to the fullest. Even for those who find much to complain about in life, at least enjoy the complaining. It may be your only chance to get it all out.

The longer I live, the more precious every moment becomes. There are so many items on my bucket list that it is impossible to accomplish them all. More than anything, I want to enjoy the special people who populate my life. They are the ones who make every precious breath feel worthwhile.

FINAL GIFT

Do not mourn my passing
whenever it shall occur

Instead
keep me deep within you
by taking qualities I possess
you find of value,
make them your own
...then pass my essence
to future generations,
    ensuring in some way
I will live forever

An Afterthought

EVOLUTION OF THE PROCESS

Younger & Wiser was assembled from the contents of two leather briefcases filled with scattered writings collected over a period of more than thirty years. A few poems had already been typed, but most were scribbled on wrinkled grocery bags, hotel memo pads, cocktail napkins, backs of business cards, and an assortment of other mangy-looking paper products. The briefcase excavation also unearthed a rather large collection of wisdom phrases stockpiled from a myriad of sources. It took more than a year just to sort through the unmanageable mess and enter all the poems and prose into a computer.

During that year of sorting, it felt like I was moving closer to myself all the time, as the collection of prose and poetry chronicled most of the twists and turns my life had taken over a major stretch of time. These diverse writings had seen me through a multitude of friendships, career moves, travel adventures, love affairs, family deaths, and personal tragedies. My writer mind had observed me make some excellent decisions and some big mistakes, even chronicling the struggle of recovery from a near-death experience in a major automobile accident. I had witnessed seismic shifts in world and national politics, and of course, September 11, 2001. While all these events felt totally unique as they occurred, upon reflection I began to sense a trail of parallel occurrences has transpired in every human era dating back to prehistoric times.

After preparing hundreds of poems and wisdom phrases, it was time to distill the chaotic conglomeration into a somewhat coherent manuscript. Somewhere in the midst of this organizational phase, a flashback to the birthplace of my entire creative process occurred. It was freshman English class at the University of Michigan. Freshman English was a required class, and we were given the choice of taking *Shakespeare* or *Creative Writing 101*. At that time I was more a fan of Jimi Hendrix than Shakespeare, so choosing *Creative Writing* was automatic. Little did I know, this class was about to revolutionize my world. If I could find the teacher who introduced me to creative writing, I would give her a huge hug of gratitude. Each day, she simply gave us an ongoing choice of subjects and told us to write. At first I was flabbergasted. Actually I was paralyzed, having been trained in school to wait for rules and restrictions before writing anything. It seemed impossible to know how to start. Our teacher literally instructed us:

"No Rules - Just Write!"

Once the paralysis wore off, I started writing. Once I started writing, I couldn't stop. That class opened my mind to the existence of creative freedom, which soon became a preferred lifestyle. Without freshman English class, I may never have become a writer and may never have allowed a creative thought to pass through my mind without first strangling it with rules.

My first flirtation with writing poetry began two years later, the summer after my first major illness. As I recovered by trekking across a variety of New York's glorious Montauk beaches, poetry simply rose up from my soul, flowed into my hand, and appeared on paper. It was as if someone else was writing from inside my skin. I learned to always carry some paper and a pen, never knowing when inspiration would erupt from my inner volcano.

After college, my career moved into the world of entertainment, where most writing was for commercial and theatrical projects. Poetry writing was sporadic and destined for imprisonment in the dark confines of an old leather briefcase. The urge to organize those tattered sheets of paper grew over the years, eventually escalating to a loud inner scream. It took many years to finally divest myself of numerous business interests and focus on organizing a book. The addition of backstories transformed this project into a joyous adventure. It caused me to realize in my youth I craved new experiences, whereas now I crave new understandings and deeper relationships. It also clarified that I am often more affected by what happens to others than to myself. Witnessing the tragedies and suffering of others has always aroused my compassionate nature and urged me to be of service.

One of my briefcases contained a sheet of paper with a short list of possible book titles accumulated over the years. None of the names on the tired sheet of paper enthralled me, which destroyed any hope of making a quick decision. As I read and reread all the poems, reviewing the older ones caused me to become increasingly aware of how young and surprisingly thoughtful I was when I started writing poetry. This led to the hope I have become continually wiser while growing older. The clichéd phrase *"older and wiser"* repeated in my mind, until composing the backstory for *Educated Sweat*, when a yellow light flashed the phrase *"younger and wiser"* inside my eyes. I immediately knew I had a title.

Looking back on my youth, I wish I had been wiser when younger, and now that I am a bit wiser, the wish is to be younger. I know I'm not alone in these sentiments, so hopefully we can all become younger and wiser by remaining youthful and flexible in our minds as we age. My core motivation for writing poetry is captured by the words of legendary psychodramatist J.L. Moreno, who said:

> *"More important than poetry itself is its result.*
> *One poem invokes a hundred heroic acts."*

A number of selections chosen for this book represent an unquenchable desire to inspire others to be a part of healing the worldwide suffering and divisiveness that currently prevails. My everlasting wish is for all who read *Younger & Wiser* to somehow be enriched by it. Hopefully my words will lead to many heroic acts, especially those that spread love and kindness.

ABOUT THE AUTHOR

Nationally acclaimed game-show host Gene Jones has spent his life inspiring others to achieve creative excellence. From seminars on innovation to more than twenty-five years of professional speech writing, the breadth of Jones's eclectic career in the world of entertainment spans more than four decades. Throughout those years, Jones has also enjoyed success as a professional juggler, fire-eater, game-show host, producer, director, radio personality, arts administrator, and television sports commentator.

From 1983-1990, Jones served as Associate Editor of the *Guinness Book of World Records*. He also appeared on numerous national television shows as their official spokesperson and world record judge. Directly as a result of his work with the *Guinness Book of World Records,* Jones created the ingenious *GIMME A HINT!*® *Trivia Game Show.* Touring nationwide, he has performed this comedic theatrical game show more than 2500 times since then.

In addition to hosting game shows, Jones currently teaches seminars on the Art of Breakthrough Thinking and the Art of Presentation, while often writing speeches for his many corporate and private clients. He has also received the Friendship Award from the United Nations for his concert performances with crystal bowls.

Jones has written everything from radio commercials to murder mysteries, but his brilliantly unique backstory poetry in *Younger & Wiser*—which bridges the gap between literary memoir and eclectic verse—is the missing link of literary expression. It is poetry for both purist and casual reader alike.

Penned over the course of Jones's extensive career, often in exotic locations around the world, the poems of *Younger & Wiser* were collected in leather briefcases that became their home for decades before being dusted off and distilled into passionate reflections brimming with wisdom and humor.

To learn more about the author, who channeled his colorful professional life and miraculous personal growth into a new form of literary expression, please visit his websites:

www.gimmeahint.com
www.triviation.com

Made in the USA
San Bernardino, CA
15 March 2017